CRISTIANO RONALDO

PORTUGUESE FOOTBALLER

MR VIVEK KUMAR PANDEY

Made with ♥ on the Notion Press Platform
www.notionpress.com

Contents

Foreword

Short Biography Of Cristiano Ronaldo About His Life Style,Career & Football History etc .During Writing This Book No Character, No Religion And No Caste Are Harmed. It's Only For Study Purpose.

Preface

Author biography in English :

MY NAME IS VIVEK KUMAR PANDEY . I WAS BORN IN 30 SEP 2002,I AM FROM SURAT GUJARAT INDIA.MY DREAM WAS TO BE GOOD WRITERS ,MY FAMILY SUPPORTED ME TO SUCCESSFUL AND I CAN DO IT MY SELF.How do I write? That is a question, I believe, that can be honestly answered by me."CELEBRATING YOUNGEST WRITER AWARD WINNER IN GUJARAT 1ST RANK" MR PANDEY JI . I may think I did a good job writing something. The reader is the one who decides the quality of my writing. I do find writing to be natural to me and therefore find it to be a real challenge. My trick as a challenged writer is to do the best I can and know that I am happy with the final outcome. It may take a while to do my best and there may be quite a few problems I run into along the way.

I am not a greedy person those who are thinking about me and my self I never tried it anyone people suffering from sadness ,I trying to get promoted people suffering from happiness and joy in your Life Time. Now in current situation in India and also world people are unemployed and have no many but our indian governor help to people to get free food from ration card , i also take part in leadership team ,i am Motivational speaker , Film script writer. There was my two dream firstly writer and secondly actor & also my own film is upcoming soon i done almost completely completed script for my film .I AM GOING TO SAY WORD OF HEART TOUCH OUT PLEASE READ IT" , firstly i thanks my father he supports me in this field they always getting inspired me by own his words and behavior ,they always said that he was a biggest person in the world in future and also they purchase fruit and chocolate for me in anytime & anyway , firstly my father buy him then call me Vivek you want a chocolate i will say yes papa but how many tell me ,papa: you tell me how much i buy him i told 1 or 2 chocolate but my father purchase whole the boxes of chocolate and they get suprised me.

MY FATHER WAS BORN IN " 20 SEPTEMBER" 1971 IN INDIA.

1) MY FATHER FAVORITE CLOTHES IS KURTA PAIJMA AND ALSO STYLES SHOE

2) FAVORITE SINGER IS KISHORE DA

3) FAVORITE STATE GUJARAT AND KOLKATA , HIS VILLAGE IN BIHAR

4) FAVORITE COLOR BLACK AND WHITE

THEY ALSO LOVE cricket like IPL and one day t-20 .they also like watching a News daily and heard the song daily ,they also interested in tik tok video but in current time tik tok is banned in india but also few videos are in you tube. In lockdown time my family and me very enjoy day daily. my father play daily ludo with his sister and son, daughter.they always loved tea and coffee anytime call me . I make it tea for my father but some reason after the April to june they are suffering from fever and cough , weakness on 6 June 2020 my father death. they not told me say bye bye his life. After death of 6 June on 10 june my mom and dad anniversary.but my father is Best in the world they can do anything for me please take care of father and respect it of your parents.

ONE

CRISTIANO RONALDO

- **Cristiano Ronaldo**

Cristiano Ronaldo was born 5 February 1985 is a Portuguese professional footballer who plays as a forward and captains the Portugal national team. He is currently a free agent. Widely regarded as one of the greatest players of all time, Ronaldo has won five Ballon d'Or awards and four European Golden Shoes, the most by a European player. He has won 32 trophies in his career, including seven league titles, five UEFA Champions Leagues, and the UEFA European Championship. Ronaldo holds the records for most appearances (183), goals (140), and assists (42) in the Champions League, goals in the European Championship (14), international goals (118), and joint-most international appearances (196). He is one of the few players to have made over 1,100 professional career appearances, and has scored over 800 official senior career goals for club and country. He is the only male player to score in five World Cup tournaments.

Ronaldo began his senior career with Sporting CP, before signing with Manchester United in 2003, at age 18, winning the FA Cup in his first season. He would also go on to win three consecutive

Premier League titles, the Champions League and the FIFA Club World Cup; at age 23, he won his first Ballon d'Or. Ronaldo was the subject of the then-most expensive association football transfer when he signed for Real Madrid in 2009 in a transfer worth €94 million (£80 million), where he won 15 trophies, including two La Liga titles, two Copa del Rey, and four Champions Leagues, and became the club's all-time top goalscorer. He won back-to-back Ballons d'Or in 2013 and 2014, and again in 2016 and 2017, and was runner-up three times behind Lionel Messi, his perceived career rival. In 2018, he signed for Juventus in a transfer worth an initial €100 million (£88 million), the most expensive transfer for an Italian club and for a player over 30 years old. He won two Serie A titles, two Supercoppa Italiana trophies and a Coppa Italia, before returning to United in 2021. He left in 2022.

Ronaldo made his international debut for Portugal in 2003 at the age of 18 and has since earned over 190 caps, making him Portugal's most-capped player. With more than 100 goals at international level, he is also the nation's all-time top goalscorer. Ronaldo has played in and scored at 11 major tournaments; he scored his first international goal at Euro 2004, where he helped Portugal reach the final. He assumed captaincy of the national team in July 2008. In 2015, Ronaldo was named the best Portuguese player of all time by the Portuguese Football Federation. The following year, he led Portugal to their first major tournament title at Euro 2016, and received the Silver Boot as the second-highest goalscorer of the tournament. He also led them to victory in the inaugural UEFA Nations League in 2019, receiving the top scorer award in the finals, and later received the Golden Boot as top scorer of Euro 2020.

One of the world's most marketable and famous athletes, Ronaldo was ranked the world's highest-paid athlete by Forbes in 2016 and 2017 and the world's most famous athlete by ESPN from 2016 to 2019. Time included him on their list of the 100 most influential people in the world in 2014. He is the first footballer and the third sportsman to earn US$1 billion in his career.

- **Cristiano Ronaldo Early life**

Cristiano Ronaldo dos Santos Aveiro was born on 5 February 1985 in the São Pedro parish of Funchal, the capital of the Portuguese island of Madeira, and grew up in the nearby parish of Santo António. He is the fourth and youngest child of Maria Dolores dos Santos Viveiros da Aveiro, a cook, and José Dinis Aveiro, a municipal gardener and part-time kit man. His great-grandmother on his father's side, Isabel da Piedade, was from the island of São Vicente, Cape Verde. He has one older brother, Hugo, and two older sisters, Elma and Liliana Cátia "Katia". His mother revealed that she wanted to abort him due to poverty, his father's alcoholism, and having too many children already, but her doctor refused to perform the procedure. Ronaldo grew up in an impoverished Catholic Christian home, sharing a room with all his siblings.

As a child, Ronaldo played for Andorinha from 1992 to 1995, where his father was the kit man, and later spent two years with Nacional. In 1997, aged 12, he went on a three-day trial with Sporting CP, who signed him for a fee of £1,500. He subsequently moved from Madeira to Alcochete, near Lisbon, to join Sporting's youth academy. By age 14, Ronaldo believed he had the ability to play semi-professionally and agreed with his mother to cease his education to focus entirely on football. While popular with other students at school, he had been expelled after throwing a chair at his teacher, who he said had "disrespected" him. One year later, he was diagnosed with tachycardia, a condition that could have forced him to give up playing football. Ronaldo underwent heart surgery where a laser was used to cauterise multiple cardiac pathways into one, altering his resting heart rate. He was discharged from the hospital hours after the procedure and resumed training a few days later.

- **Cristiano Ronaldo memorabilia at Sporting CP's museum**

At age 16, Ronaldo was promoted from Sporting's youth team by first-team manager László Bölöni, who was impressed with his dribbling. He subsequently became the first player to play for the club's under-16, under-17 and under-18 teams, the B team and the first team, all within a single season. A year later, on 29 September 2002, Ronaldo made his debut in the Primeira Liga, against Braga and on 7 October, he scored two goals against Moreirense in their 3–0 win. Over the course of the 2002–03 season, his representatives suggested the player to Liverpool manager Gérard Houllier and Barcelona president Joan Laporta. Manager Arsène Wenger, who was interested in signing Ronaldo, met with him at Arsenal's stadium in November to discuss a possible transfer.

Manchester United manager Alex Ferguson was determined to acquire Ronaldo on a permanent move urgently, after Sporting defeated United 3–1 at the inauguration of the Estádio José Alvalade in August 2003. Initially, United had planned to sign Ronaldo and loan him back to Sporting for a year. Having been impressed by him, the United players urged Ferguson to sign him. After the game, Ferguson agreed to pay Sporting £12.24 million for what he considered to be "one of the most exciting young players" he had ever seen. A decade after his departure from the club, in April 2013, Sporting honoured Ronaldo by selecting him to become their 100,000th member.

- **Cristiano Ronaldo 2003–2007: Development and breakthrough**

"There have been a few players described as 'the new George Best' over the years, but this is the first time it's been a compliment to me."Former Manchester United player George Best hails the 18-year-old Cristiano Ronaldo in 2003.

Ronaldo's move to Manchester United was completed on 12 August 2003, too late for the 2003 FA Community Shield but in time for their game against Bolton Wanderers on the opening day of the 2003–04 season, and made him the first Portuguese player to sign for the club. His transfer fee made him, at the time, the most expensive teenager in English football history. Although he requested the number 28, his number at Sporting, he received the squad number 7 shirt, which had previously been worn by such United players as George Best, Eric Cantona and David Beckham. Wearing the number 7 became an extra source of motivation for Ronaldo. A key element in his development during his time in England proved to be Ferguson, of whom he later said: "He's been my father in sport, one of the most important and influential factors in my career."

- **Cristiano Ronaldo playing for Manchester United against**

Ronaldo made his debut as a substitute in a 4–0 home win over Bolton Wanderers in the Premier League on 16 August 2003, and received a standing ovation when he came on for Nicky Butt. His performance earned praise from Best, who hailed it as "undoubtedly the most exciting debut" he had ever seen. Ronaldo scored his first goal for Manchester United with a free-kick in a 3–0 win over Portsmouth on 1 November. Three more league goals followed in the second half of the campaign, the last of which came against Aston Villa on the final day of the season, a match in which he also received the first red card of his career. Ronaldo ended his first season in English football by scoring the opening goal in United's 3–0 win over Millwall in the 2004 FA Cup Final, earning his first trophy. BBC pundit Alan Hansen described him as the star of the final. The British press had been critical of Ronaldo during the season for his "elaborate" step-overs in trying to beat opponents, but teammate Gary Neville said he was "not a show pony, but the real thing", and predicted he would become a world-class player.

"He has got the tricks and party pieces, we know that, but they're not much good unless there is something at the end of it all. We still have to remember, of course, that the lad is only 19 years of age. Considering that, you have to say he has got massive talent. His feet are mesmerising at times, and if he can couple that with some consistently good crossing, the future looks frightening."Former

BBC pundit Alan Hansen commenting on Ronaldo after his first season.

Ronaldo scored United's 1,000th Premier League goal on 29 October 2004, their only goal in a 4–1 loss to Middlesbrough.A few weeks later, he signed a new contract with the club that extended his previous deal by two years to 2010. At the start of 2005, Ronaldo played two of his best matches of the 2004–05 season, producing a goal and an assist against Aston Villa and scoring twice against rivals Arsenal. He played the full 120 minutes of the 2005 FA Cup Final against Arsenal, which ended in a goalless draw; although Ronaldo scored his attempt in the penalty shoot-out, United lost 5–4. Ronaldo won his second trophy in English football, the Football League Cup, after scoring the third goal in United's 4–0 final win over Wigan Athletic.

During his third season in England, Ronaldo was involved in several incidents. He had a one-match ban imposed on him by UEFA for a "one-fingered gesture" towards Benfica fans, and was sent off in the Manchester derby (a 3–1 defeat) for kicking Manchester City's former United player Andy Cole. Ronaldo clashed with a teammate, striker Ruud van Nistelrooy, who took offence at the winger's showboating style of play. Following the 2006 FIFA World Cup, in which he was involved in an incident where club teammate Wayne Rooney was sent off, Ronaldo publicly asked for a transfer, lamenting the lack of support he felt he had received from the club over the incident. United denied the possibility of him leaving the club.

Although his World Cup altercation with Rooney resulted in Ronaldo being booed throughout the 2006–07 season, it proved to be his breakout year, as he broke the 20-goal barrier for the first time and won his first Premier League title. An important factor in this success was his one-to-one training by first-team coach René Meulensteen, who taught him to make himself more unpredictable, improve his teamwork, call for the ball and capitalise on goalscoring opportunities rather than waiting for the chance to score the aesthetically pleasing goals for which he was already known. He scored three consecutive braces at the end of December, against Aston Villa (a win that put United on top of the league), Wigan and Reading. Ronaldo was named the Premier League Player of the Month in November and December, becoming only the third player to receive consecutive honours.

- **Cristiano Ronaldo playing during the 2006–07 Premier League season**

At the quarter-final stage of the 2006–07 UEFA Champions League, Ronaldo scored his first goals in his 30th match in the competition, scoring twice in a 7–1 win over Roma. He subsequently scored four minutes into the first semi-final leg against Milan, which ended in a 3–2 win, but was marked out of the second leg as United lost 3–0 at the San Siro. He also helped United reach the 2007 FA Cup Final, but the final against Chelsea ended in a 1–0 defeat. Ronaldo scored the only goal in the Manchester derby on 5 May (his 50th goal for the club), as United won their first league title in four years. As a result of his performances, he amassed a host of personal awards for the season. He won the Professional Footballers' Association's Player's Player, Fans' Player and Young Player of the Year awards, as well as the Football Writers' Association's Footballer of the Year award, becoming the first player to win all four main PFA and FWA honours. His wages were raised to £120,000 a week as part of a five-year contract extension. Ronaldo was named runner-up to Kaká for the 2007 Ballon d'Or, and came third, behind Kaká and Lionel Messi, in the running for the 2007 FIFA World Player of the Year award.

Ronaldo scored his first hat-trick for United in a 6–0 win against Newcastle United on 12 January 2008, which put United top of the league table. On 19 March, he captained United for the first time in a home win over Bolton and scored both goals in a 2–0 win. His second goal was his 33rd of the campaign, surpassing George Best's total of 32 goals in the 1967–68 season, setting the club's new single-season record by a midfielder.

His 31 league goals earned him the Premier League Golden Boot, as well as the European Golden Shoe, which made him the first winger to win the latter award. He additionally received the PFA Players' Player of the Year and FWA Footballer of the Year awards for the second consecutive season. In the knockout stage of the Champions League, Ronaldo scored the decisive goal against Lyon to help United advance to the quarter-finals 2–1 on aggregate; while playing as a striker, he scored with a header in the 3–0 aggregate win over Roma. United reached the final against Chelsea in Moscow, where, despite his opening goal being negated by an equaliser and his penalty kick being saved in the shoot-out, United emerged victorious. As the Champions League top scorer, Ronaldo was named the UEFA Club Footballer of the Year.

Ronaldo scored a total of 42 goals in all competitions during the 2007–08 season, his most prolific campaign during his time in England. He missed three matches after headbutting a Portsmouth player at the start of the season, an experience he said taught him not to let opponents provoke him. As rumours circulated of Ronaldo's interest in moving to Real Madrid, United filed a tampering complaint with governing body FIFA over Madrid's alleged pursuit of their player, but they declined to take action. FIFA president Sepp Blatter asserted that the player should be allowed to leave his club, describing the situation as "modern slavery". Despite Ronaldo publicly agreeing with Blatter, he remained at United for another year.

- **Cristiano Ronaldo 2008–2009: Ballon d'Or and continued success**

Ahead of the 2008–09 season, on 7 July, Ronaldo underwent ankle surgery, which kept him out of action for 10 weeks. Following his return, he scored his 100th goal in all competitions for United with the first of two free kicks in a 5–0 win against Stoke City on 15 November,which meant he had now scored against all 19 opposition teams in the Premier League at the time. At the close of 2008,

Ronaldo helped United win the 2008 FIFA Club World Cup in Japan, assisting the final-winning goal against Liga de Quito and winning the Silver Ball in the process. With his 2008 Ballon d'Or and 2008 FIFA World Player of the Year, Ronaldo became United's first Ballon d'Or winner since Best in 1968, and the first Premier League player to be named the FIFA World Player of the Year.

His match-winning goal in the second leg against Porto, a 40-yard strike, earned him the inaugural FIFA Puskás Award, presented by FIFA in recognition of the best goal of the year. he later called it the best goal he had ever scored. United advanced to the final in Rome, where he made little impact in United's 2–0 defeat to Barcelona. Ronaldo ended his time in England with nine trophies, as United claimed their third successive league title and a Football League Cup. He finished the campaign with 26 goals in all competitions, 16 goals fewer than the previous season, in four more appearances. His final goal for United came on 10 May 2009 with a free kick in the Manchester derby at Old Trafford.

- **Cristiano Ronaldo Real Madrid**

As his usual number 7 was unavailable, Ronaldo wore number 9 during his debut season at Madrid. After Raúl departed the club, Ronaldo was handed the number 7 shirt before the 2010–11 season.

Ahead of the 2009–10 season, Ronaldo joined Real Madrid for a world record transfer fee at the time of £80 million (€94 million). His contract, which ran until 2015, was worth €11 million per year and contained a €1 billion buy-out clause. At least 80,000 fans attended his presentation at the Santiago Bernabéu, surpassing the 25-year record of 75,000 fans who had welcomed Diego Maradona at Napoli. Since club captain Raúl already wore the number 7 , Ronaldo received the number 9 shirt, which was presented to him by former Madrid player Alfredo Di Stéfano.

- **Cristiano Ronaldo 2009–2013: World record transfer and La Liga title**

Ronaldo made his La Liga debut against Deportivo La Coruña on 29 August, scoring a penalty in a 3–2 home win. He scored in each of his first four league games, the first Madrid player to do so. His first Champions League goals for the club followed with two free kicks in the first group match against Zürich. His strong start to the season was interrupted when he suffered an ankle injury in October while on international duty, which kept him sidelined for seven weeks. A week after his return, he received his first red card in Spain in a match against Almería. Midway through the season, Ronaldo finished second in the 2009 Ballon d'Or and the 2009 FIFA World Player of the Year awards, behind Messi. He finished the season with 33 goals in all competitions, including a hat-trick in a 4–1 win against Mallorca on 5 May 2010, his first in La Liga, and became Real Madrid's highest goalscorer that season. Although Ronaldo helped amass a club record 96 points in the league, he did not win a trophy in his first season.

Following Raúl's departure, Ronaldo was given the number 7 shirt for Madrid before the 2010–11 season. His subsequent return to his Ballon d'Or-winning form was epitomised when, for the first time in his career, he scored four goals in a single match during a 6–1 rout against Racing Santander on 23 October. Ronaldo subsequently scored further hat-tricks against Athletic Bilbao, Levante, Villarreal and Málaga. Despite his performances, he did not make the top three in the inaugural 2010 FIFA Ballon d'Or. During a historic series of four Clásicos against rivals Barcelona in April 2011, Ronaldo scored twice to equal his personal record of 42 goals in all competitions.

Though he failed to score in either leg of the Champions League semi-finals as Madrid were eliminated, he equalised from the penalty spot in the return league game and scored the match-winning goal in the 103rd minute of the 2011 Copa del Rey Final, winning his first trophy in Spain. His two goals in the last match of the season against Almería made him the first player in La Liga to score 40 goals. In addition to the Pichichi Trophy, Ronaldo won the European Golden Shoe for a second time, becoming the first player to win the award in different leagues.

Ronaldo scored 46 league goals during the La Liga championship success in his third season in Spain.During the following season, Ronaldo achieved a new personal best of 60 goals in all competitions. He finished as runner-up to Messi for the 2011 FIFA Ballon d'Or, after scoring hat-tricks against Real Zaragoza, Rayo Vallecano, Málaga, Osasuna and Sevilla, the last of which put Madrid on top of the league by the season's midway point.

Ronaldo found greater team success in the league, helping Madrid win their first league title in four years with a record 100 points. Following a hat-trick against Levante as Madrid further increased their lead over Barcelona, he scored his 100th league goal for Madrid in a 5–1 win over Real Sociedad on 24 March 2012, a milestone he reached in just 92 matches across three seasons, breaking the previous club record held by Ferenc Puskás. Another hat-trick in the Madrid derby against Atlético Madrid brought his total to 40 league goals, equalling his record of the previous season. His final league goal of the season, against Mallorca, took his total to 46 goals, four short of the new record set by Messi, though he became the first player to score against all 19 opposition teams in a single La Liga season.

Ronaldo began the 2012–13 season by lifting the 2012 Supercopa de España, his third trophy in Spain. With a goal in each leg, he helped Madrid win the Spanish Super Cup on away goals following a 4–4 aggregate draw against Barcelona. Although Ronaldo publicly commented that he was unhappy with a "professional issue" within the club, prompted by his refusal to celebrate his 150th goal for Madrid,his goalscoring rate did not suffer. After netting a hat-trick, including two penalties, against Deportivo, he scored his first hat-trick in the Champions League in a 4–1 win over Ajax. Four days later, he became the first player to score in six successive Clásicos when he hit a brace in a 2–2 draw at Camp Nou. His performances again saw Ronaldo voted second in the running for the 2012 FIFA Ballon d'Or, behind four-time winner Messi.

Following the 2012–13 winter break, Ronaldo captained Madrid for the first time in an official match, scoring twice to lift 10-man Madrid to a 4–3 win over Sociedad on 6 January. He subsequently became the first non-Spanish player in 60 years to captain Madrid in El Clasico on 30 January, a match which also marked his 500th club appearance. Three days prior, he had scored his 300th club goal as part of a perfect hat-trick against Getafe. He scored his 200th goal for Madrid on 8 May in a 6–2 win against Málaga, reaching the landmark in 197 games. He helped Madrid reach the 2013 Copa del Rey Final by scoring twice in El Clásico, which marked the sixth successive match at Camp Nou in which he had scored, a club record. In the final, he headed the opening goal of an eventual 2–1 extra time defeat to Atlético, but was shown a red card for violent conduct.

In the first knockout round of the Champions League, Ronaldo faced his former club Manchester United for the first time. After scoring the equaliser in a 1–1 draw at home, he scored the winning goal in a 2–1 win on his first return to Old Trafford. He did not celebrate scoring against his former club as a mark of respect. After scoring three goals against Galatasaray in the quarters, he scored Madrid's only goal in the 4–1 away defeat to Borussia Dortmund in the semi-finals and Real were eliminated at the semi-final stage for the third consecutive year despite a 2–0 win in the second leg.

Ronaldo scored a record 17 UEFA Champions League goals during the 2013–14 season en route to La Décima.At the start of the 2013–14 season, Ronaldo signed a new contract that extended his stay by three years to 2018, with a salary of €17 million net, making him briefly the highest-paid player in football. He was joined at the club by winger Gareth Bale, whose world record transfer fee of €100 million surpassed the fee Madrid had paid for Ronaldo four years prior. Together with striker Karim Benzema, they formed an attacking trio popularly dubbed "BBC", an acronym of Bale, Benzema and Cristiano, and a play on the name of the British public service broadcaster, the British Broadcasting Corporation (BBC).

By late November, Ronaldo had scored 32 goals from 22 matches for both club and country, including hat-tricks against Galatasaray, Sevilla, Real Sociedad, Northern Ireland, and Sweden. He ended 2013 with 69 goals in 59 appearances, his highest year-end goal tally. He received the 2013 FIFA Ballon d'Or, an amalgamation of the Ballon d'Or and the FIFA World Player of the Year award, for the first time in his career.

Concurrently with his individual achievements, Ronaldo enjoyed his greatest team success in Spain to date, as he helped Madrid win La Décima, their tenth European Cup. His goal in a 3–0 home win over Dortmund took his total for the season to 14 goals, equalling the record Messi had set two years before. After hitting a brace in a 4–0 defeat of Bayern Munich at the Allianz Arena, he scored from the penalty spot in the 120th minute of the 4–1 final win over Atlético, becoming the first player to score in two European Cup finals for two different winning teams. His overall performance in the final was subdued as a result of patellar tendinitis and related hamstring problems, which had plagued him in the last months of the campaign. Ronaldo played the final against medical advice, later commenting: "In your life you do not win without sacrifices and you must take risks". As the competition's top goalscorer for the third time, with a record 17 goals, he was named the UEFA Best Player in Europe.

In the Copa del Rey, Ronaldo helped Madrid reach the final by scoring two penalties against Atlético at the Vicente Calderón, the first of which meant he had now scored in every single minute of a 90-minute football match. His continued issues with his knee and thigh caused him to miss the final, where Madrid defeated Barcelona 2–1 to claim the trophy.Ronaldo scored 31 goals in 30 league games, which earned him the Pichichi and the European Golden Shoe, receiving the latter award jointly with Liverpool striker Luis Suárez. Among his haul was his 400th career goal, in 653 appearances for club and country, which came with a brace against Celta Vigo on 6 January; he dedicated his goals to compatriot Eusébio, who had died two days before. A last-minute, back-heeled volley scored against Valencia on 4 May (his 50th goal in all competitions) was recognised as the best goal of the season by the Liga Nacional de Fútbol Profesional, which additionally named Ronaldo the Best Player in La Liga.

During the 2014–15 season, Ronaldo set a new personal best of 61 goals, starting with both goals in Madrid's 2–0 win over Sevilla in the UEFA Super Cup.He subsequently achieved his best-ever goalscoring start to a league campaign, with 15 goals in the first eight rounds. His record 23rd La Liga hat-trick, scored against Celta Vigo on 6 December, made him the fastest player to reach 200 goals in La Liga, reaching the milestone in 178th matches.

After winning the 2014 FIFA Club World Cup, Ronaldo received the 2014 Ballon d'Or, joining Johan Cruyff, Michel Platini and Marco van Basten as a three-time recipient. Madrid finished in second place in La Liga and exited at the semi-final stage in the Champions League. In the latter competition, Ronaldo extended his run of scoring away to a record 12 matches with his strike in a 2–0 win against Schalke 04. He scored both of his side's goals in the semi-finals against Juventus, where Madrid were eliminated 3–2 on aggregate. With 10 goals, he finished as top scorer for a third consecutive season, alongside Messi and Neymar. On 5 April, he scored five goals in a game for the first time in his career, including an eight-minute hat-trick, in a 9–1 rout of Granada. His 300th goal for his club followed three days later in a 2–0 win against Rayo Vallecano.Subsequent hat-tricks against Sevilla, Espanyol and Getafe took his number of hat-tricks for Madrid to 31, surpassing Di Stéfano's club record of 28. He finished the season with 48 goals, winning a second consecutive Pichichi and the European Golden Shoe for a record fourth time.

- **Cristiano Ronaldo 2015–2017: All-time Madrid top scorer**

At the start of his seventh season at Madrid, the 2015–16 campaign, Ronaldo became the club's all-time top scorer, first in the league and then in all competitions. His five-goal haul in a 6–0 away win over Espanyol on 12 September took his tally in La Liga to 230 goals in 203 games, surpassing the club's previous record holder, Raúl. A month later, on 17 October, he again surpassed Raúl when he scored the second goal in a 3–0 defeat of Levante at the Bernabéu to take his overall total for the club to 324 goals. Ronaldo also became the all-time top scorer in the Champions League with a hat-trick in the first group match against Shakhtar Donetsk, having finished the previous season level with Messi on 77 goals.Two goals against Malmö FF in a 2–0 away win on 30 September saw him reach the milestone of 500 career goals for club and country. He subsequently became the first player to score double figures in the competition's group stage, setting the record at 11 goals, including another four-goal haul against Malmö.

By March 2016, Ronaldo had scored 252 goals in 228 matches in La Liga to become the competition's second-highest goalscorer.Ronaldo's four goals in a 7–1 home win over Celta de Vigo on 5 March 2016 took his total to 252 goals in La Liga, becoming the competition's second-highest scorer in history behind Messi. He scored a hat-trick against VfL Wolfsburg to send his club into the Champions League semi-finals. The treble took his tally in the competition to 16 goals, making him the top scorer for the fourth consecutive season and the fifth overall.

Suffering apparent fitness issues, Ronaldo gave a poorly-received performance in the final against Atlético, in a repeat of the 2014 final, though his penalty in the subsequent shoot-out secured Madrid's 11th victory. For the sixth successive year, he ended the season having scored over 50 goals across all competitions. For his efforts during the season, he received the UEFA Best Player in Europe Award for a second time.

Ronaldo missed Madrid's first three matches of the 2016–17 season, including the 2016 UEFA Super Cup against Sevilla, as he continued to rehabilitate the knee injury he suffered against France in the Euro 2016 final. On 15 September, he did not celebrate his late free kick equaliser against Sporting CP in the Champions League, with Ronaldo stating post match that "they made me who I am".

On 7 November, his contract was updated for the second time and extended by three years to 2021.

On 19 November, he scored a hat-trick in a 3–0 away win against Atlético, making him the all-time top scorer in the Madrid derby with 18 goals. On 15 December, Ronaldo scored his 500th club career goal in the 2–0 win over Club América in the semi-finals of the 2016 FIFA Club World Cup. He then scored a hat-trick in the 4–2 win over Japanese club Kashima Antlers in the final. Ronaldo finished the tournament as top scorer with four goals and was also named player of the tournament. He won the 2016 Ballon d'Or, his fourth, and the inaugural 2016 The Best FIFA Men's Player, a revival of the former FIFA World Player of the Year, largely owing to his success with Portugal in winning Euro 2016.

- **Cristiano Ronaldo in 2016 Champions League title celebrations in Madrid**

In the 2016–17 UEFA Champions League quarter-finals against Bayern in April, Ronaldo scored both goals in a 2–1 away win which saw him make history by becoming the first player to reach 100 goals in UEFA club competition. In the second leg of the quarter-finals, Ronaldo scored a 'perfect' hat-trick and reached his 100th Champions League goal, becoming the first player to do so as Madrid again defeated Bayern 4–2 after extra-time. On 2 May, Ronaldo scored another hat-trick as Madrid defeated Atlético 3–0 in the Champions League semi-final first leg. On 17 May, Ronaldo overtook Jimmy Greaves as the all-time top scorer in the top five European leagues, scoring twice against Celta de Vigo. He finished the season with 42 goals in all competitions as he helped Madrid to win their first La Liga title since 2012.In the Champions League Final, Ronaldo scored two goals in a 4–1 victory over Juventus to take him to 12 goals for the season, making him the competition's top goalscorer for the fifth straight season (sixth overall), as well as the first player to score in three finals in the Champions League era; the second goal was the 600th of his senior career. Madrid also became the first team to win back-to-back finals in the Champions League era.

- **Cristiano Ronaldo 2017–2018: Fifth Ballon d'Or and fifth Champions League win**

At the start of the 2017–18 season, Ronaldo scored Madrid's second goal in the 80th minute of a 3–1 win over Barcelona in the first leg of the 2017 Supercopa de España at Camp Nou; however, he was sent off two minutes later and missed the second leg. On 23 October, his performances throughout 2017 saw him awarded The Best FIFA Men's Player award for the second consecutive year. On 6 December, he became the first player to score in all six Champions League group stage matches with a curling strike at home to Dortmund. A day later, Ronaldo won the 2017 Ballon d'Or, receiving his fifth-time award on the Eiffel Tower in Paris. On 16 December, he scored a free kick winner, as Madrid won their second Club World Cup in a row by beating Grêmio in the final. On 3 March 2018, he scored two goals in a 3–1 home win over Getafe, his first being his 300th La Liga goal in his 286th appearance, making him the fastest player to reach this landmark and only the second player to do so after Messi. On 18 March, he reached his 50th career hat-trick, scoring four goals in a 6–3 win against Girona.

- **Cristiano Ronaldo in the 2018 UEFA Champions League Final**

On 3 April, Ronaldo scored the first two goals in a 3–0 away win against Juventus in the quarter-finals of the 2017–18 UEFA Champions League, with his second goal being an acrobatic bicycle kick. Described as a "PlayStation goal" by Juventus defender Andrea Barzagli, with Ronaldo's foot approximately 7 ft 7 in (2.31 m) off the ground, it garnered him a standing ovation from the opposing fans in the stadium as well as a plethora of plaudits from peers, pundits and coaches. On 11 April, he scored in the second leg at home to Juventus, a 98th-minute injury time penalty in a 3–1 defeat, meaning

Madrid advanced 4–3 on aggregate. It was his tenth goal against Juventus, a Champions League record against a single club. In the final on 26 May, Madrid defeated Liverpool 3–1, winning Ronaldo his fifth Champions League title, the first player to do so. He finished as the top scorer of the tournament for the sixth consecutive season with 15 goals. After the final, Ronaldo referred to his time with Madrid in the past tense, sparking speculation that he could leave the club.

Despite months of negotiation to sign a new Real Madrid contract, on 10 July 2018, Ronaldo signed a four-year contract with Italian club Juventus after completing a €100 million transfer, which included an additional 12 million in other fees and solidarity contributions to Ronaldo's youth clubs. The transfer was the highest ever for a player over 30 years old, and the highest paid by an Italian club. Upon signing, Ronaldo cited his need for a new challenge as his rationale for departing Madrid, but later attributed the transfer to the lack of support he felt was shown by club president Florentino Pérez.

- **Cristiano Ronaldo 2018–2020: Adjustment and consecutive Series A titles**

On 18 August, Ronaldo made his debut in a 3–2 away win against Chievo Verona. On 16 September, Ronaldo scored his first two goals for Juventus in his fourth appearance in a 2–1 home win over Sassuolo in Serie A; his second was the 400th league goal of his career. On 19 September, in his first Champions League match for Juventus, he was sent off in the 29th minute for "violent conduct", his first red card in 154 tournament appearances. Ronaldo became the first player in history to win 100 Champions League matches, setting up Mario Mandžukić's winner in a 1–0 home win over Valencia, which sealed Juventus's passage to the knock-out stages of the competition.

In December, he scored his tenth league goal of the season, from the penalty spot, netting the final goal in a 3–0 away win over

Fiorentina. After placing second in both the UEFA Men's Player of the Year and The Best FIFA Men's Player for the first time in three years, behind Luka Modrić, Ronaldo performances in 2018 also saw him voted runner-up for the 2018 Ballon d'Or, finishing once again behind his former teammate. Ronaldo won his first trophy with the club on 16 January 2019, the 2018 Supercoppa Italiana, after he scored the only goal from a header against AC Milan.

On 10 February, Ronaldo scored in a 3–0 win over Sassuolo, the ninth consecutive away game in which he had scored in the league, equalling Giuseppe Signori's single season Serie A record of most consecutive away games with at least one goal. On 12 March, Ronaldo scored a hat-trick in a 3–0 home win against Atlético in the second leg of the Champions League round of 16, helping Juventus overcome a two-goal deficit to reach the quarter-finals. The following month, he scored his 125th goal in the competition, opening the scoring in a 1–1 away draw in the quarter-final first leg against Ajax on 10 April.

In the second leg in Turin on 16 April, he scored the opening goal, but Juventus eventually lost the match 2–1 and were eliminated from the competition. On 20 April, Ronaldo played in the scudetto clinching game against Fiorentina, as Juventus won their eighth successive title after a 2–1 home win, thereby becoming the first player to win league titles in England, Spain and Italy.On 27 April, he scored his 600th club goal, the equaliser in a 1–1 away draw against Derby d'Italia rivals Inter Milan. Ending his first Serie A campaign with 21 goals and 8 assists, Ronaldo won the inaugural Serie A award for Most Valuable Player.

- **Cristiano Ronaldo playing for Juventus against Torino during the 2019–20 season**

Ronaldo scored his first goal of the 2019–20 season in a 4–3 home league win over Napoli on 31 August 2019. On 23 September, he came in 3rd place for the Best FIFA Men's Player Award. On 1 October, he reached several milestones in Juventus's 3–0 Champions

League group stage win over Bayer Leverkusen: he scored in a 14th consecutive season, equalling Raúl and Messi's record; he broke Iker Casillas' record for most Champions League wins of all time, and equalled Raúl's record of scoring against 33 different opponents. On 6 November in a 2–1 away win against Lokomotiv Moscow, he equalled Paolo Maldini as the second-most capped player in UEFA club competitions with 174 appearances.

On 18 December, Ronaldo leapt to a height of 8 ft 5 in (2.57 m), higher than the crossbar, to head the winning goal in a 2–1 away win against Sampdoria. He scored his first Serie A hat-trick on 6 January 2020, in a 4–0 home win against Cagliari. His 56th career hat-trick, he became only the second player after Alexis Sánchez to score hat-tricks in the Premier League, La Liga and Serie A. On 2 February, he scored twice from the penalty spot in a 3–0 home win over Fiorentina, equalling David Trezeguet's club record of scoring in nine consecutive league games, and broke the record six days later by scoring in his tenth consecutive league game, a 2–1 away defeat to Hellas Verona. On 22 February, Ronaldo scored for a record-equalling 11th consecutive league game, alongside Gabriel Batistuta and Fabio Quagliarella, in what was his 1,000th senior professional game, a 2–1 away win against SPAL.

On 22 June, he scored a penalty in a 2–0 away win over Bologna, overtaking Rui Costa to become the highest scoring Portuguese player in Serie A history. On 4 July, he scored his 25th league goal from a free kick in a 4–1 home win over rivals Torino, becoming the first Juventus player to achieve this milestone since Omar Sívori in 1961; the goal was also his first from a free kick with the club after 43 attempts. On 20 July, Ronaldo scored twice in a 2–1 home win over Lazio; his first goal was his 50th in Serie A. He became the second-fastest player to reach this landmark, after Gunnar Nordahl, and the first player in history to reach 50 goals in the Premier League, La Liga and Serie A. With his brace, he also reached 30 league goals for the season, becoming just the third player in Juventus's history to reach that milestone in a season. Moreover, he became the oldest player, at the age of 35 years and 166 days, to score over 30 goals in one of the five top European leagues since Ronnie Rooke with Arsenal in 1948.

On 26 July, Ronaldo scored the opening goal in a 2–0 home win over Sampdoria as Juventus were crowned Serie A champions for a ninth consecutive time. He finished his second league campaign with 31 goals, making him the second-highest goalscorer in the league behind only European Golden Shoe winner Ciro Immobile, with 36 goals. On 7 August, Ronaldo scored a brace in a 2–1 home win against Lyon in the second leg of the Champions League round of 16, which saw him finish the season with 37 goals in all competitions; the tally allowed him to break Borel's club record of 36 goals in a single season. Despite the win, the tie finished 2–2 on aggregate and Juventus were eliminated from the competition on the away goals rule.

- **Cristiano Ronaldo 2020–2021: 100 Juve goals**

On 20 September 2020, Ronaldo scored in Juventus's opening league match of the season, a 3–0 home win over Sampdoria. On 1 November, having taken nearly three weeks to recover from COVID-19, he returned to action against Spezia; he came off the bench in the second half and scored within the first three minutes, before scoring a second goal from the penalty spot in an eventual 4–1 away win. On 2 December, he scored a goal against Dynamo Kyiv in a Champions League group stage match, his 750th senior career goal. Ronaldo played his 100th match in all competitions for Juventus on 13 December, scoring two penalties in a 3–1 away win over Genoa in the league to bring his goal tally to 79.

On 20 January 2021, Juventus won the 2020 Supercoppa Italiana after a 2–0 win against Napoli, with Ronaldo scoring the opening goal. On 2 March, he scored a goal in a 3–0 win over Spezia in his 600th league match, to become the first player to score at least 20 goals in 12 consecutive seasons in the top five leagues of Europe. On 14 March, he scored his 57th career hat-trick in a 3–1 away win over Cagliari. On 12 May, Ronaldo scored a goal in a 3–1 away win over

Sassuolo to reach his 100th goal for Juventus in all competitions on his 131st appearance, becoming the fastest Juventus player to achieve the feat. With Juventus's victory in the 2021 Coppa Italia Final on 19 May, Ronaldo became the first player in history to win every major domestic trophy in England, Spain and Italy. Ronaldo ended the season with 29 league goals, winning the Capocannoniere award for highest goalscorer and becoming the first footballer to finish as top scorer in the English, Spanish and Italian leagues.

On 22 August, Ronaldo started the first game of the new season on the bench, coming on as a substitute for Álvaro Morata in a 2–2 draw against Udinese, scoring a goal that was ruled out by VAR. Though manager Massimiliano Allegri confirmed it was his decision due to Ronaldo's fitness, it came amid reports Ronaldo would depart the club before the closure of the transfer window, and Ronaldo would tell Allegri he had "no intention" of remaining a Juventus player. On 26 August, Ronaldo and his agent Jorge Mendes reached a verbal agreement with Manchester City over personal terms, but the club pulled out of the deal the following day due to the overall cost of the transfer. On the same day, it was confirmed that City's rivals Manchester United, Ronaldo's former club, were in advanced talks to sign him, while former manager Alex Ferguson and several ex-teammates had been in contact to persuade him to re-sign for United.

- **Cristiano Ronaldo Return to Manchester United**

On 27 August 2021, Manchester United announced they had reached an agreement with Juventus to re-sign Ronaldo, subject to agreement of personal terms, visa and medical. The transfer was for an initial €12.85 million, with a two-year contract plus an optional year, and was confirmed on 31 August. Ronaldo was given the number 7 shirt after Edinson Cavani agreed to switch to 21. The first 24 hours of Ronaldo's shirt sales was reported to have broken the all-time record following a transfer, overtaking Messi after his move to Paris Saint-Germain.

Ronaldo in a Premier League match against Newcastle in September 2021, his first game back at Manchester United.On 11 September, Ronaldo made his second debut at Old Trafford, scoring the opening two goals in a 4–1 league victory against Newcastle United. On 29 September, he scored a last-minute winner in United's 2–1 victory at home to Villarreal in the Champions League, and overtook Iker Casillas as the player with the most appearances in the competition. In the next Champions League fixture on 20 October, Ronaldo again scored a last minute winner, helping United overturn a two-goal deficit in a 3–2 home victory against Atalanta, and scored both goals, including a last minute equalizer, in the reverse fixture against Atalanta on 2 November. On 23 November, Ronaldo became the first player to score in five consecutive matches of a Champions League campaign for an English club, after opening United's 2–0 victory away against Villarreal, with his six goals being crucial to United's qualifying for the round of 16 as group winners. On 2 December, Ronaldo netted two goals in a 3–2 home league win against Arsenal, which saw him surpass 800 career goals.

The following month, after enduring a fractured relationship with his teammates and interim manager Ralf Rangnick, his performances and his team's declined during the season, with Ronaldo equalling his worst goalscoring run since 2010 during his time with Real Madrid, being two months without scoring a goal, before scoring his first goal in the new year, opening United's 2–0 win home against Brighton & Hove Albion on 15 February 2022. Following a hamstring injury, which saw him miss the Manchester derby against Manchester City, Ronaldo made his return from injury on 12 March, scoring a hat-trick in a 3–2 victory against Tottenham Hotspur, which saw him pass Josef Bican's record for goals scored in professional football with 807 career goals, although the Football Association of the Czech Republic claimed that Bican had scored 821 career goals. On 16 April, Ronaldo scored his 50th club hat-trick in a 3–2 win over Norwich City. On 23 April, he scored his 100th Premier League goal in a 3–1 defeat to Arsenal. After scoring in the following matches against Chelsea and Brentford, he was named the Premier League Player of the Month for April.

He finished the season with 24 goals in all competitions, 18 of those goals being in the Premier League, making him the third-highest goalscorer in the league behind Golden Boot winners Mohamed Salah and Son Heung-min, being named in the Premier League Team of the Year and the winner of United's Sir Matt Busby Player of the Year award, given to the club's best player from the previous season. however, with United finishing in a disappointing sixth place and qualifying for the UEFA Europa League, Ronaldo went trophyless for the first time since 2010.

- **Cristiano Ronaldo 2022: Final season**

After growing dissatisfaction with the direction of United on and off the field, Ronaldo missed the club's pre-season tour of Thailand and Australia due to family reasons, amid reports of his desire to leave to join a club competing in the Champions League, despite incoming manager Erik ten Hag insisting that he was not for sale and was part of the club's plans. His agent Jorge Mendes began negotiating with various clubs for a transfer on loan or on a free transfer, including Bayern Munich, Paris Saint-Germain and Chelsea, with the latter club's new owner Todd Boehly being keen on a possible transfer. However, due to his age, overall cost of a transfer and high wages demands, multiple European clubs rejected the opportunity to sign him, including Chelsea after their manager Thomas Tuchel did not approve his signing.

- **Cristiano Ronaldo in a Premier League match against Brighton & Hove Albion**

Having failed to secure a transfer, Ronaldo lost his place in the starting lineup to Marcus Rashford and Anthony Martial, only featuring in Europa League matches. He scored his first goal in the competition aged 37, converting a penalty to make it 2–0 against Sheriff Tiraspol on 15 September. On 2 October, Ronaldo was an unused substitute in United's 6–3 loss to Manchester City, with ten Hag saying that he refused to bring him on out of "respect for his big career". On 9 October, Ronaldo came on as a substitute and scored his 700th career club goal in a 2–1 win against Everton. Ten days later, Ronaldo refused to be brought on as a substitute during a home game against Tottenham and left the ground before the full-time whistle.

Ten Hag punished him by dropping him from the squad for an upcoming fixture with Chelsea, and made him train separately from the first team. Following discussions with the manager, Ronaldo returned to training and started in United's home win over Sheriff on 27 October, scoring the third goal and ensuring United's qualification to the Europa League knockout stage. Ten Hag named Ronaldo as captain for a 3–1 defeat to Aston Villa on 6 November, saying that Ronaldo was "an important part of the squad, we are happy with him and now he has to take even more of the leader role". Ronaldo then missed United's following matches before the World Cup break, with Ten Hag saying that Ronaldo was ill.

On 14 November, an interview with Piers Morgan was published, where Ronaldo said that he felt "betrayed" by Ten Hag and senior executives who wanted Ronaldo to leave the club, and accused the club of doubting him regarding the illness of his daughter that led him to miss pre-season, adding that he did not respect ten Hag "because he doesn't show respect for me", leading him to be disappointed with the communication of the club. Ronaldo claimed that ten Hag deliberately provoked him by first leaving him on the bench against City, and then wanting to bring him on in the final moments against Tottenham, but added that he regretted his decision to leave early.

He also questioned the appointment of Rangnick the previous season as he was a "sporting director and not even a coach". On the club itself, Ronaldo stated there was "no evolution" since the departure of former manager Alex Ferguson in 2013, despite expecting changes in "technology, infrastructure". Ronaldo claimed that the Glazer family "did not care about the club" as he never spoke with them, and described United as a "marketing club". Following the interview, which aired in two-parts on 16 and 17 November, United began seeking legal action over whether Ronaldo had breached his contract, and were looking to terminate his contract. On 22 November, Ronaldo's contract was terminated by mutual agreement with immediate effect.

- **Cristiano Ronaldo International career**

Ronaldo began his international career with Portugal under-15 in 2001. During his international youth career, Ronaldo would represent the under-15, under-17, under-20, under-21 and under-23 national sides, amassing 34 youth caps and scoring 18 goals overall.

Aged 18, Ronaldo made his first senior appearance for Portugal in a 1–0 win over Kazakhstan on 20 August 2003, coming on as a half-time substitute for Luís Figo. He was subsequently called up for UEFA Euro 2004, held in his home country, and scored his first international goal in a 2–1 group stage loss to eventual champions Greece, his eighth appearance for Portugal. After converting his penalty in a shoot-out against England in the quarter-finals, he helped Portugal reach the final by scoring the opening goal in a 2–1 win over the Netherlands.He was featured in the team of the tournament, having provided two assists in addition to his two goals.

Ronaldo was Portugal's second-highest scorer in their qualification group for the 2006 FIFA World Cup with seven goals. During the tournament, he scored his first World Cup goal against Iran with a penalty kick in Portugal's second match of the group stage. At the age of 21 years and 132 days, Ronaldo became the youngest ever goalscorer for Portugal at a World Cup finals. In Portugal's infamously dirty round of 16 match against the Netherlands, Ronaldo was forced off injured in the first half after a tackle from Dutch defender Khalid Boulahrouz.

Following Portugal's 1–0 win, Ronaldo accused Boulahrouz of intentionally trying to injure him, although he recovered in time to play in the next game. In Portugal's quarter-final against England, Ronaldo's Manchester United teammate Wayne Rooney was sent off for stamping on Portugal defender Ricardo Carvalho. Although the referee later clarified that the red card was only due to Rooney's infraction, the English media speculated that Ronaldo had influenced his decision by aggressively complaining, after which he was seen in replays winking at Portugal's bench following Rooney's dismissal. Ronaldo went on to score the vital winning penalty during the shoot-out which sent Portugal into the semi-finals. Ronaldo was subsequently booed during their 1–0 semi-final defeat to France. FIFA's Technical Study Group overlooked him for the tournament's Best Young Player award and handed it to Germany's Lukas Podolski, citing his behaviour as a factor in the decision. Following the 2006 World Cup, Ronaldo would go on to represent Portugal in four qualifying games for Euro 2008, scoring two goals in the process.

- **Cristiano Ronaldo in 2007–2012: Assuming the captaincy**

One day after his 22nd birthday, Ronaldo captained Portugal for the first time in a friendly game against Brazil on 6 February 2007, as requested by Portuguese Football Federation (FPF) president Carlos Silva, who had died two days earlier. Ahead of Euro 2008, he was given the number 7 shirt for the first time. While he scored eight goals in the qualification,the second-highest tally, he scored just one goal in the tournament, netting the second goal of their 3–1 win in the group stage match against the Czech Republic; in the same game, he also set-up Portugal's third goal in injury time, which was scored by Quaresma, and was named man of the match for his performance. Portugal were eliminated in the quarter-finals with a 3–2 loss against eventual finalists Germany.

After Portugal's unsuccessful performance at Euro 2008, Luiz Felipe Scolari was replaced as coach by Carlos Queiroz, formerly the assistant manager at United. Queiroz made Ronaldo the squad's permanent captain in July 2008. Ronaldo failed to score a single goal in the qualification for the 2010 World Cup, as Portugal narrowly avoided a premature elimination from the tournament with a play-off victory over Bosnia and Herzegovina. In the group stage of the World Cup, he was named man of the match in all three matches, against Ivory Coast, North Korea and Brazil. His only goal of the tournament came in their 7–0 rout of North Korea, which marked his first international goal in 16 months.Portugal's World Cup ended with a 1–0 loss against eventual champions Spain in the round of 16.

Ronaldo scored seven goals in the qualification for Euro 2012, including two strikes against Bosnia and Herzegovina in the play-offs, to send Portugal into the tournament, where they were drawn in a "group of death". In the last group stage game against the Netherlands, Ronaldo scored twice to secure a 2–1 win. He scored a header in the quarter-final against the Czech Republic to give his team a 1–0 win. In both games against the Netherlands and the Czech Republic he was named man of the match. After the semi-finals against Spain ended scoreless, Portugal were eliminated in the penalty shoot-out. Ronaldo did not take a penalty as he had been slated to take the unused fifth slot. Ronaldo's own teammate, Nani, said that Ronaldo "demanded" to take the last penalty. As the joint top scorer with three goals, alongside five other players, he was again included in the team of the tournament.

- **Cristiano Ronaldo 2012–2016: All-time Portugal top scorer and European champion**

During the qualification for the 2014 World Cup, Ronaldo scored a total of eight goals. A qualifying match on 17 October 2012, a 1–1 draw against Northern Ireland, earned him his 100th cap. His first international hat-trick also came against Northern Ireland, when he scored three times in a 15-minute spell of a 4–2 qualifying win on 6 September 2013. After Portugal failed to qualify during the regular campaign, Ronaldo scored all four of the team's goals in the play-offs against Sweden, billed as a battle between Ronaldo and Zlatan Ibrahimović, which ensured their place at the tournament.

His hat-trick in the second leg took his international tally to 47 goals, equaling Pauleta's record. Ronaldo subsequently scored twice in a 5–1 friendly win over Cameroon on 5 March 2014 to become his country's all-time top scorer.

Ronaldo took part in the tournament despite suffering from patellar tendinitis and a related thigh injury, potentially risking his career. Ronaldo later commented: "If we had two or three Cristiano Ronaldos in the team I would feel more comfortable. But we don't." Despite ongoing doubts over his fitness, being forced to abort practice twice, Ronaldo played the full 90 minutes of the opening match against Germany, although he was unable to prevent a 4–0 defeat. After assisting an injury-time 2–2 equaliser against the United States, he scored a late match-winning goal in a 2–1 win over Ghana. His 50th international goal made him the first Portuguese to play and score in three World Cups. Portugal were eliminated from the tournament at the close of the group stage on goal difference.

- **Cristiano Ronaldo leaps in the air in Portugal's Euro 2016 quarter-final match against Poland**

Ronaldo scored five goals, including a hat-trick against Armenia, in the qualification for Euro 2016. With the only goal in another win over Armenia on 14 November 2014, he reached 23 goals in the UEFA European Championship, including qualifying matches, to become the competition's all-time leading goalscorer. At the start of the tournament, Ronaldo failed to convert his chances in Portugal's draws against Iceland and Austria, despite taking 20 shots on goal. In the latter match, he overtook Figo as Portugal's most capped player with his 128th international appearance, which ended scoreless after he missed a penalty in the second half. With two goals in the last match of the group stage, a 3–3 draw against Hungary, Ronaldo became the first player to score in four European Championships, having made a record 17 appearances in the tournament. Although placed third in their group behind Hungary and Iceland, his team qualified for the knockout round as a result of the competition's newly expanded format, despite not winning any of their games.

In Portugal's first knockout match, Ronaldo's only attempt on goal was parried by Croatia's goalkeeper Danijel Subašić into the path of Ricardo Quaresma, whose finish then secured a 1–0 win late in extra time. After his team progressed past Poland on penalties, with Ronaldo scoring Portugal's opening penalty, he became the first player to participate in three European Championship semi-finals. he scored the opener in a 2–0 win against Wales, equalling Michel Platini as the competition's all-time top scorer with nine goals.

In the final against hosts France, Ronaldo was forced off after just 25 minutes following a challenge from Dimitri Payet, despite multiple treatments and attempts to play on, he was stretchered off the pitch and replaced by Quaresma. During extra time, substitute Eder scored in the 109th minute to earn Portugal a 1–0 victory. As team captain, Ronaldo lifted the trophy in celebration of his country's first triumph in a major tournament. He was awarded the Silver Boot as the joint second-highest goalscorer, with three goals and three assists, and was named to the team of the tournament for the third time in his career.

- **Cristiano Ronaldo 2016–2018: Post-European Championship victory and World Cup**

Following the Euro 2016 success, Ronaldo played his first professional match on his home island of Madeira on 28 March 2017 at age 32, opening a 2–3 friendly defeat to Sweden at the Estádio dos Barreiros. With the goal, he tied with Miroslav Klose on 71 goals as the third-highest scoring European in international football.

In Portugal's opening match of the 2017 FIFA Confederations Cup against Mexico on 17 June, Ronaldo set up Quaresma's opening goal in a 2–2 draw. Three days later, he scored in a 1–0 win over hosts Russia. On 24 June, he scored from a penalty in a 4–0 win over New Zealand, which saw Portugal top their group and advance to the semi-finals of the competition; with his 75th international goal, Ronaldo also equalled Sándor Kocsis as the second-highest European international goalscorer of all-time, behind only Ferenc Puskás. He was named man of the match in all three of Portugal's group stage matches. Ronaldo left the competition early; after Chile defeated Portugal 3–0 on penalties in the semi-finals, he was allowed to return home to be with his newborn children, and missed Portugal's third-place play-off match in which Portugal defeated Mexico 2–1 after extra time.

- **Cristiano Ronaldo evades an Iran defender in the group stage of the 2018 World Cup**

On 31 August 2017, Ronaldo scored a hat-trick in a 5–1 win in a 2018 World Cup qualifying match over the Faroe Islands, which saw him overtake Pelé and equal Hussein Saeed as the joint-fifth-highest goalscorer in international football with 78 goals. These goals brought his tally in the World Cup qualifiers to 14, equalling Predrag Mijatović's record for most goals in a single UEFA qualifying campaign, and also saw him break the record for the most goals scored in a European qualifying group, overtaking the previous record of 13 goals set by David Healy and Robert Lewandowski. Ronaldo's hat-trick took his World Cup qualifying goals total to 29, making him the highest scorer in UEFA qualifiers, ahead of Andriy Shevchenko, and the highest goalscorer in World Cup qualifying and finals matches combined with 32 goals, ahead of Miroslav Klose.Ronaldo later added to this tally by scoring a goal against Andorra in a 2–0 win.

On 15 June 2018, Ronaldo became the oldest player to score a hat-trick in a FIFA World Cup match, helping Portugal secure a 3–3 draw against Spain (his third goal a 30-yard curling free kick with two minutes remaining) in their opening match. In doing so, he became the first Portuguese player to score a goal in four World Cups and one of four players of any nationality to do so. On 20

June, Ronaldo scored the only goal in a 1–0 win against Morocco, breaking Puskás‘ record as the highest European goalscorer of all-time, with 85 international goals. In the final group match against Iran on 25 June, Ronaldo missed a penalty in an eventual 1–1 draw which saw Portugal progress to the second round as group runners-up behind Spain. On 30 June, Portugal were eliminated following a 2–1 defeat to Uruguay in the last 16. For his performances in the tournament, Ronaldo was named in the World Cup Dream Team.

- **Cristiano Ronaldo 2018–2020: Nations League title and 100 international goals**

After the World Cup, Ronaldo missed six international matches, including the entire league phase of the 2018–19 UEFA Nations League, but played for hosts Portugal in the inaugural Nations League Finals in June 2019. In the semi-finals on 5 June, he scored a hat-trick against Switzerland to reach the final. Upon scoring the opening goal, he became the first player to score in 10 consecutive international competitions, breaking the record he previously shared with Ghana’s Asamoah Gyan. In the final of the tournament four days later, Portugal defeated the Netherlands 1–0.

On 10 September 2019, Ronaldo scored four goals in a 5–1 away win over Lithuania in a Euro 2020 qualifying match in the process, he overtook Robbie Keane (23 goals) as the player with most goals in the UEFA European Championship qualifying, setting a new record with 25 goals. He also set a new record for scoring against the most national teams, 40, while also completing his eighth international hat-trick.

On 14 October, he scored his 700th senior career goal for club and country from the penalty spot, in his 974th senior career appearance, a 2–1 away loss to Ukraine in a Euro 2020 qualifier. On 17 November, Ronaldo scored his 99th international goal in a 2–0 win over Luxembourg, leading Portugal to qualify for Euro 2020. On 8 September 2020, Ronaldo scored his 100th and 101st international goals in a 2–0 away win over Sweden in a 2020–21 UEFA Nations

League match, becoming only the second male player ever to achieve this milestone (after Ali Daei of Iran) and the first in Europe. On 13 October, the FPF announced that Ronaldo tested positive for COVID-19 while being asymptomatic. By 30 October, Ronaldo had recovered.

- **Cristiano Ronaldo 2021–present: All-time international top goalscorer**

On 15 June 2021, Ronaldo scored twice in Portugal's first game of Euro 2020, a 3–0 win against Hungary in Budapest. This took him to a total of 11 European Championship goals, two clear of Michel Platini, as the all-time top goalscorer in the competition's history.He also became the first player to score at five Euros, and in eleven consecutive tournaments. The brace made Ronaldo the oldest player to score two goals in a match in the competition, and the oldest player to score for Portugal at a major tournament. On 23 June, he scored two penalties in Portugal's 2–2 draw with France in their final group stage match, equalling Daei's record of 109 international goals. On 27 June, Portugal were eliminated following a 1–0 loss against Belgium in the round of 16. Ronaldo finished the tournament with five goals and one assist, earning him the Golden Boot.

- **Cristiano Ronaldo during a group stage game against Uruguay at the 2022 World Cup**

On 1 September, Ronaldo scored two headed goals, with his second coming seconds before the full-time whistle, in a 2–1 home win against the Republic of Ireland in a World Cup qualifier at the Estádio Algarve, which saw him pass Daei to become the sole record holder. On 9 October, he scored the opening goal in a 3–0 friendly win over Qatar at the Estádio Algarve; with his 181st international appearance, he also overtook Sergio Ramos's record for the most international caps received by a European player. In the following match against Luxembourg on 12 October, also played at the Estádio Algarve, Ronaldo scored a hat-trick in a 5–0 win for Portugal, and became the first player to score 10 hat-tricks in men's international football.

Ronaldo was named in Portugal's squad for the 2022 FIFA World Cup in Qatar, making it his fifth World Cup. On 24 November, in Portugal's opening match against Ghana, Ronaldo scored a penalty kick and became the first male player to score in five different World Cups. In the last group game against South Korea, Ronaldo received criticism from his own coach for his reaction at being substituted. He was dropped from the starting line-up for Portugal's last 16 match against Switzerland, marking the first time since Euro 2008 that he had not started a game for Portugal in a major international tournament, and the first time Portugal had started a knockout game without Ronaldo in the starting line-up at an international tournament since Euro 2000. He came off the bench late on as Portugal won 6–1, their highest tally in a World Cup knockout game since the 1966 World Cup, with Ronaldo's replacement Gonçalo Ramos scoring a hat-trick. Portugal employed the same strategy in the quarter-finals against Morocco, with Ronaldo again coming off the bench. They lost 1–0, with Morocco becoming the first CAF nation to reach the semi-finals.

- **Cristiano Ronaldo Style of play**

A versatile attacker, Ronaldo is capable of playing on either wing as well as through the centre of the pitch, and, while ostensibly right-footed, is very strong with both feet. Tactically, Ronaldo has undergone several evolutions throughout his career. While at Sporting and during his first season at Manchester United, he was typically deployed as a traditional winger on the right side of midfield, where he regularly looked to deliver crosses into the penalty area. In this position, he was able to use his pace and acceleration, agility and technical skills to take on opponents in one-on-one situations. Ronaldo became noted for his dribbling and flair, often displaying an array of tricks and feints, such as the step overs and so-called 'chops' that became his trademark. he has also been known to use the flip-flap.

Ronaldo controlling the ball on his chest during a 2010–11 La Liga game against Almería. At his peak, he was known for his exceptional speed and athleticism.As Ronaldo matured, he underwent a major physical transformation, developing a muscular body type that allowed him to retain possession of the ball under pressure, and strong legs that enabled an outstanding jumping ability. His strength and jumping ability, combined with his elevation, heading accuracy and height of 1.87 m (6 ft 1+1⁄2 in), give him an edge in winning aerial duels. These attributes allow him to function as a target-man and make him an aerial goal threat in the penalty area; consequently, many of his goals have been headers. Allied with his increased stamina and work-rate, his goalscoring ability improved drastically on the left wing where he was given the positional freedom to move into the centre to finish attacks. He has also increasingly played a creative role for his team, often dropping deep to pick up the ball, participate in the build-up of plays and create chances for his teammates, courtesy of his vision and passing ability.

In his final seasons at United, Ronaldo played an even more attacking and central role, functioning both as a striker and as a supporting forward, or even as an attacking midfielder on occasion. He developed into a prolific goalscorer, capable of finishing well both inside the penalty area and from distance with an accurate and powerful shot, courtesy of his striking ability. An accurate penalty kick taker, he also became a set piece specialist, renowned for his powerful, bending free kicks.

When taking free kicks, Ronaldo is known for using the knuckleball technique, which was developed by Juninho Pernambucano. He also adopts a trademark stance before striking the ball, which involves him standing with his legs far apart. Regarding Ronaldo's unique style of taking free kicks, former Manchester United assistant manager Mike Phelan commented:

"People used to put the ball down, walk away, run up and hit it. He brought in a more dynamic showmanship. He places the ball down, the concentration level is high, he takes his certain amount of steps back so that his standing foot is in the perfect place to hit the ball in the sweet spot. He is the ultimate showman. He has that slight arrogance. When he pulls those shorts up and shows his thighs, he is saying 'All eyes on me' and this is going in. He understands the marketing side of it. The way he struts up and places it; the world is watching him."

At Real Madrid, Ronaldo continued to play a more offensive role, while his creative and defensive duties became more limited, although not entirely diminished. Initially deployed as a centre forward by managers Manuel Pellegrini and José Mourinho, he was later moved back onto the left wing, though in a free tactical role; this position allowed him to drift into the centre at will to get onto the end of crosses and score, or draw out defenders with his movement off the ball and leave space for teammates to exploit. Madrid's counter-attacking style of play also allowed him to become a more efficient and consistent player, as evidenced by his record-breaking goalscoring feats. While he mainly drew praise in the media for his prolific goalscoring, Ronaldo also demonstrated his ability as an effective creator in this role.

This unique role has been described by pundits as that of a "false", "attacking", or "goalscoring winger", as Ronaldo effectively almost functioned as a striker at times with his central runs into the penalty area, despite actually playing on the left flank. From 2013 onwards, under manager Carlo Ancelotti, he effectively adapted his style to the physical effects of ageing with increasingly reduced off-the-ball movement and general involvement, completing fewer dribbles and passes per game, and instead focusing on short-distance creating and goalscoring. Since 2017, Ronaldo adapted his style of play yet again to become more of a free-roaming centre forward under manager Zinedine Zidane, a role in which he continued to excel and maintain a prolific goalscoring record; in this position, he earned praise in the media for his intelligent movement both on and off the ball, positional sense, link-up play and finishing, as well as his ability to lose or anticipate his markers, find space in the box and score from few touches or opportunities.

In his first season at Juventus, Ronaldo continued to play in a variety of different attacking roles under manager Massimiliano Allegri, depending on whom he was partnered with. While he had occupied an increasingly offensive role in his final years at Real Madrid, at times he functioned in a free role at Juventus, either as a lone striker or in his trademark role on the left wing, in a 4–2–3–1 or 4–3–3 formation, in which he often switched positions with Mario Mandžukić. In this role, he was also given licence to drop deep or even out wide onto the right flank to receive the ball, and be more involved in the build-up of plays; as such, aside from scoring goals himself, he began to take on opponents and create chances for other players with greater frequency than he had in his final seasons with Real Madrid. Off the ball, he was also capable of creating space for teammates with his movement and attacking runs into the box, or finishing off chances with his head or feet by getting onto the end of his teammates' crosses. On occasion he also played in an attacking partnership alongside Mandžukić in a 4–3–1–2, 4–4–2, or 3–5–2 formation. He continued to play a similar role in his second season with the club under manager Maurizio Sarri.

- **Cristiano Ronaldo is widely regarded**

Ronaldo is widely regarded as one of the two best players of his generation, alongside Lionel Messi. Winning his first Ballon d'Or in 2008 by a record-high vote count at age 23, over the next decade Ronaldo has often featured in debates concerning who is the greatest player in history. Acclaimed for his prolific and consistent goal-scoring, he is considered a decisive player who is also a game changer, especially in important and high-pressured situations.

Fans of Real Madrid (left; Ronaldo's then current club) and Manchester United (right; Ronaldo's then former club as he joined United again in 2021) wearing Ronaldo's 7 shirt at the 2017 UEFA

Super Cup

Ronaldo is noted for his work ethic, elite body conditioning and dedication to improvement on the training pitch, as well being regarded as a natural leader. On his longevity and "extraordinary commitment to physical preparation", Adam Bate of Sky Sports said: "Dedication is a huge part of staying at the top and Ronaldo's focus is perhaps unparalleled within the game." While stating they were stylistically different players who shared an equal desire to score goals, former Brazil international Ronaldo praised Cristiano's approach to training, arguing that "there are so few players who take care of their body like he does. I trained because I had to, he does it because he loves it."

His drive and determination to succeed are fuelled by a desire to be talked about alongside other greats such as Pelé and Diego Maradona once retiring. He is credited, along with his compatriot, coach José Mourinho, with inspiring changing fortunes of Portuguese football in 2010s and 2020s. At times, he has been criticised for simulating when tackled. He was also occasionally criticised early in his career by manager Alex Ferguson, teammates and the media for being a selfish or overly flamboyant player. Jonathan Wilson of The Guardian opined that Ronaldo had made Juventus, who he joined aged 33 in 2018, weaker, due to "his relative immobility" in his mid-30s, even if his personal goal-scoring output remained high.

During his career, Ronaldo has also been described as having an "arrogant image" on the pitch, with Ronaldo stating that he had become a "victim" because of how he was portrayed in the media. He is often seen moaning, gesticulating and scowling while trying to inspire his team to victory, with Ronaldo insisting that his competitive nature should not be mistaken for arrogance. His managers, teammates and various journalists have said that this reputation has caused an unfair image of him.

- **Cristiano Ronaldo Goal celebrations**

Scoring goals is the hardest part of the game. Some players don't even score in training! What more can you say about him? He's a genius! , Roy Keane, on Cristiano Ronaldo's prolific goal-scoring record.Ronaldo has adopted several goal celebrations throughout his career, including one particular celebration which gained widespread coverage in the media, when he squatted and stared directly into a camera on the sidelines of the pitch with his hand on his chin. After scoring a goal, he usually celebrates with a "storming jump" and "turn", before "landing in spread-eagled fashion" into his "signature power stance", while usually simultaneously exclaiming "Sí" (Spanish and Italian for "yes"). This trademark celebration has been dubbed the "Sii" in the media.

- **Messi–Ronaldo rivalry**

Ronaldo with Lionel Messi before an international friendly between Portugal and Argentina in 2011Both players have scored in multiple UEFA Champions League finals and have regularly broken the 50-goal barrier in a single season. Sports journalists and pundits regularly weigh the individual merits of both players in an attempt to argue who they believe is the best player in modern football or in the history of the game. It has been compared to several sports rivalries, among them the Muhammad Ali–Joe Frazier rivalry in boxing, the Borg–McEnroe rivalry in tennis and the Senna–Prost rivalry from Formula One motor racing. Some commentators choose to analyse the differing physiques and playing styles of the two, Part of the debate revolves around the contrasting personalities of the two players, as Ronaldo is sometimes depicted as an arrogant and theatrical showoff, while Messi is portrayed as a shy, humble character.

"It's part of my life now. People are bound to compare us. He tries to do his best for his club and for his national team, as I do, and there is a degree of rivalry with both of us trying to do the best for the teams we represent."

- **Cristiano Ronaldo commenting on his rivalry with Messi**

In a 2012 interview, Ronaldo commented on the rivalry, saying: "I think we push each other sometimes in the competition, this is why the competition is so high." Alex Ferguson, Ronaldo's manager during his time at Manchester United, opined: "I don't think the rivalry against each other bothers them. I think they have their own personal pride in terms of wanting to be the best." Messi himself denied any rivalry, saying that it was "only the media, the press, who wants us to be at loggerheads but I've never fought with Cristiano." Responding to the claims that he and Messi do not get on well on a personal level, Ronaldo commented: "We don't have a relationship outside the world of football, just as we don't with a lot of other players." Ronaldo added that in years to come he hopes they can laugh about it together, stating: "We have to look on this rivalry with a positive spirit, because it's a good thing." Representing archrivals Barcelona and Real Madrid, the two players faced each other at least twice every season in the world's biggest club game, El Clásico, which is among the world's most viewed annual sporting events.

In a debate at Oxford Union in October 2013, when asked whether FIFA president Sepp Blatter preferred Messi or Ronaldo, Blatter paid tribute to the work ethic of the Argentine before taking a swipe at Ronaldo, claiming "one of them has more expenses for the hairdresser than the other." Real Madrid demanded and promptly received a full apology. In response to Blatter's "commander" on the pitch comment, Ronaldo issued his own riposte with a mock-salute celebration after scoring a penalty against Sevilla. In August 2019, Ronaldo and Messi were interviewed while sat next to each other prior to the announcement of the UEFA Men's Player of the Year, with Ronaldo stating: "I pushed him and he pushed me as well. So it's good to be part of the history of football."

- **Cristiano Ronaldo Outside football**

The Cristiano Ronaldo Museum, Museu CR7, in Funchal, Madeira. It was opened on 15 December 2013.As his reputation grew from his time at Manchester United, Ronaldo has signed many sponsorship deals for consumer products, including sportswear, football boots; since November 2012, Ronaldo has worn the Nike Mercurial Vapor personalized CR7 edition, soft drinks, clothing, automotive lubricants, financial services, electronics, and video games. Ronaldo was featured as the cover star of EA Sports' FIFA video game FIFA 18 and was heavily involved in the game's promotion.His "Sii" goal celebration features in the FIFA series, accompanied with his own voiceover. He was also the face of Pro Evolution Soccer, appearing on the covers of the 2008, 2012 and 2013 editions of the game.

With earnings of 720 million (615 million) from 2010 to 2019, Ronaldo was ranked second in Forbes list of The Highest-Paid Athletes Of The Decade, with only boxer Floyd Mayweather Jr. earning more. Forbes twice ranked Ronaldo first on its list of the world's highest-paid football players; his combined income from salaries, bonuses and endorsements was $73 million in 2013–14 and $79 million in 2014–15.

The latter earnings saw him listed behind only Mayweather on the magazine's list of The World's Highest-Paid Athletes. In 2016, he became the first footballer to top the Forbes list of highest-earning athletes, with a total income of $88 million from his salary and endorsements in 2015–16. He topped the list for the second straight year with earnings of $93 million in 2016–17. He is the first footballer and only the third sportsman to earn $1 billion in their career. Ronaldo is one of the world's most marketable sportsmen: SportsPro rated him the fifth most marketable athlete in 2012 and eighth most marketable athlete in 2013, with Brazilian footballer Neymar topping both lists. Sports market research company Repucom named Ronaldo the most marketable and most recognised football player in the world in May 2014. He was additionally named in the 2014 Time 100, Time's annual list of the most influential people in the world. ESPN named Ronaldo the world's most famous athlete in 2016, 2017, 2018 and 2019.

- **Statue of Cristiano Ronaldo**

Ronaldo has established a strong online presence. The most popular sportsperson on social media, he counted over 500 million total followers across Facebook, Twitter and Instagram by February 2021, making him the first person to pass half a billion followers. The most-followed person on Facebook (148 million), the most-followed on Instagram (310 million) and the most-followed sportsperson on Twitter (92 million), his sponsors earned $936 million in media value across his accounts between June 2016 to June 2017. Ronaldo has released two mobile apps. In December 2011, he launched an iPhone game called Heads Up with Cristiano, created by developer RockLive, and in December 2013, he launched Viva Ronaldo, a dedicated social networking website and app. Computer security company McAfee produced a 2012 report ranking footballers by the probability of an internet search for their name leading to an unsafe website, with Ronaldo's name first on the list.

Ronaldo has been the subject of several works. His autobiography, titled Moments, was published in December 2007. His sponsor Castrol produced the television film Ronaldo: Tested to the Limit, in which he was physically and mentally tested in several areas; his physical performance was consequently subject to scrutiny by world media upon the film's release in September 2011. Cristiano Ronaldo: The World at His Feet, a documentary narrated by actor Benedict Cumberbatch, was released via Vimeo in June 2014. A documentary film directed by Anthony Wonke about his life and career, titled Ronaldo, was released on 9 November 2015.

Portuguese Prime Minister António Costa presents Indian Prime Minister Narendra Modi a signed Ronaldo shirt in January 2017 .Demand for a replica Ronaldo shirt has been high throughout his career. In 2008, Ronaldo's number 7 Manchester United shirt was the best-selling Premier League sports product. In 2015, Ronaldo's number 7 Real Madrid shirt was the second best-selling worldwide, after Messi's number 10 Barcelona shirt. In 2018, within 24 hours of his number 7 Juventus shirt being released, over 520,000 had been sold, with $62.4 million generated in one day.

Ronaldo opened a fashion boutique under the name CR7 (his initials and shirt number) on the island of Madeira in 2006 and opened a second in Lisbon in 2008. In partnership with Scandinavian manufacturer JBS Textile Group and the New York fashion designer Richard Chai, Ronaldo co-designed a range of underwear and sock line, released in November 2013. He expanded his CR7 fashion brand by launching a line of premium shirts and shoes in July 2014. In September 2015, Ronaldo released his own fragrance, "Legacy", in a partnership with Eden Parfums.

In 2007, C.D. Nacional renamed its youth campus Cristiano Ronaldo Campus Futebol (Cristiano Ronaldo Football Campus).In December 2013, Ronaldo opened a museum, Museu CR7, in his hometown of Funchal, Madeira, to house trophies and memorabilia. the museum is an official sponsor of the local football team União da Madeira. At a ceremony held at the Belém Palace in January 2014, President of Portugal Aníbal Cavaco Silva raised Ronaldo to the rank of Grand Officer of the Order of Prince Henry "to distinguish an athlete of world renown who has been a symbol of Portugal globally, contributing to the international projection of the country and setting an example of tenacity for future generations." A bronze statue of Ronaldo, designed by artist Ricardo Madeira Veloso, was unveiled in Funchal on 21 December 2014.

In June 2010, during the build-up to the World Cup, Ronaldo became the fourth footballer (after Steven Gerrard, Pelé, and David Beckham) to be represented as a waxwork at Madame Tussauds London. Another waxwork of him was presented at the Madrid Wax Museum in December 2013. In June 2015, astronomers led by David Sobral from Lisbon and Leiden discovered a galaxy which they named Cosmos Redshift 7 (CR7) in tribute to Ronaldo.

On 23 July 2016, following Portugal's triumph at Euro 2016, Madeira Airport in Funchal was renamed as Cristiano Ronaldo

International Airport. The unveiling of the rebranded terminal took place on 29 March 2017, which included a bust of his head being presented. The bust and the name change were controversial, with the lack of the bust's likeness to Ronaldo being ridiculed by comedians, including Saturday Night Live, while the name change was subject to much debate locally by some politicians and citizens, who even started a petition against the move, an action criticised by President of Madeira Miguel Albuquerque. A year later, sports website Bleacher Report commissioned sculptor Emanuel Santos to create another bust. however, this bust was never used and a new one was made by a Spanish sculptor, shown to the public on 15 June 2018.

- **Cristiano Ronaldo Personal life**

Ronaldo has had six children. He first became a father to a son, who was born on 17 June 2010 in the United States. He has full custody of the child and has not publicly revealed the identity of the mother per an agreement with her. In January 2015, Ronaldo's five-year relationship with Russian model Irina Shayk ended.

Ronaldo became a father to twins, born on 8 June 2017 in the United States via surrogacy. He is currently in a relationship with Argentine-born Spanish model Georgina Rodríguez, who gave birth to a daughter on 12 November 2017.The couple expected their second pair of twins in 2022. The male twin died during childbirth while the female twin survived.Ronaldo's father, José, died of an alcoholism-related liver condition at age 52 in September 2005 when Ronaldo was 20.

- **Cristiano Ronaldo Health**

Ronaldo has said that he does not drink alcohol, and he received libel damages over a Daily Mirror article that reported him drinking heavily in a nightclub while recovering from an injury in July 2008. He also does not have any tattoos as he regularly donates blood and bone marrow.

Ronaldo has made contributions to various charitable causes throughout his career. Television footage of the 2004 Indian Ocean earthquake and tsunami showed an eight-year-old boy survivor named Martunis wearing a Portuguese football shirt who was stranded for 19 days after his family was killed. Following this, Ronaldo visited Aceh, Indonesia, to raise funds for rehabilitation and reconstruction. After accepting undisclosed damages from a libel case against The Sun newspaper in 2008, Ronaldo donated the damages to a charity in Madeira. In 2009, Ronaldo donated £100,000 to the hospital that saved his mother's life in Madeira following her battle with cancer, so that they could build a cancer centre on the island. In support of the victims of the 2010 Madeira flood, Ronaldo pledged to play in a charity match in Madeira between Primeira Liga club Porto and players from Madeiran-based clubs Marítimo and Nacional.

In 2012, Ronaldo and his agent paid for specialist treatment for a nine-year-old Canarian boy with apparently terminal cancer. In December 2012, Ronaldo joined FIFA's "11 for Health" programme to raise awareness amongst kids of how to steer clear of conditions including drug addiction, HIV, malaria, and obesity. In January 2013, Ronaldo became Save the Children's new Global Artist Ambassador, in which he hopes to help fight child hunger and obesity. In March 2013, Ronaldo agreed to be the ambassador for The Mangrove Care Forum in Indonesia, an organisation aiming to raise awareness of mangrove conservation.

Ronaldo was named the world's most charitable sportsperson in 2015 after donating £5 million to the relief effort after the earthquake in Nepal which killed over 8,000 people.In June 2016, Ronaldo donated the entirety of his €600,000 Champions League bonus after Real Madrid won the competition.In August, Ronaldo launched CR7Selfie, a selfie app for charity to help Save the Children that lets participants take a selfie with him in one of several different outfits and poses.

In July 2017, Ronaldo was charged with fraudulently evading almost 15 million in tax between 2011 and 2014, a claim he denied at the time. In June 2018, Ronaldo was given a two-year suspended jail sentence and fined 18.8 million, later reduced to €16.8 million after reaching a deal with Spanish authorities. The sentence can be served under probation, without any jail time, so long as he does not re-offend.

Ronaldo and another man were investigated by the British Crown Prosecution Service after a 2005 rape allegation was brought forward by two women. Within days, the two women withdrew their allegation and Scotland Yard later issued a statement declaring there was not enough evidence for a prosecution.In April 2017, it was reported that Ronaldo was being investigated by the Las Vegas Police Department for an allegation by a woman that he had raped her in 2009. Documents, confirmed by Ronaldo's lawyers, state that Ronaldo paid a woman US 375,000 in a non-disclosure settlement.

Ronaldo and his lawyers issued a lengthy statement denying all accusations, describing them as an "intentional defamation campaign" with parts significantly "altered and/or completely fabricated", a claim which Der Spiegel categorically denied. In July 2019, Las Vegas prosecutors said they would not charge Ronaldo over allegations of rape; the statement added: "Based upon a review of information at this time, the allegations of sexual assault against Cristiano Ronaldo cannot be proven beyond a reasonable doubt." The same woman, in September 2018, filed a civil lawsuit in Nevada accusing Ronaldo of rape. The Daily Mirror, citing court documents, reported in 2021 that the woman sought £56 million in damages from Ronaldo.

In October 2021, federal magistrate judge Daniel Albregts recommended that the lawsuit be dismissed, citing that the woman's lawyer, Leslie Stovall, "acted in bad faith by asking for, receiving, and using Football Leaks documents to prosecute" the case, despite the documents containing "privileged communications" between Ronaldo and his lawyers. Additionally,

Albregts stated that no evidence was found of Ronaldo's lawyers having "intimidated or impeded law enforcement" during the 2010 settlement with her. In June 2022, the woman's rape lawsuit was dismissed with prejudice in the United States District Court for the District of Nevada, as district judge Jennifer A. Dorsey ruled that Stovall's repeated use of "cyber-hacked attorney-client privileged documents" were actions representing "abuses and flagrant circumvention of the proper litigation process".

TWO

FOOTBALL HISTORY

The history of football (soccer)

Football (or soccer as the game is called in some parts of the world) has a long history. Football in its current form arose in England in the middle of the 19th century. But alternative versions of the game existed much earlier and are a part of the football history.

- **history and the precursors of football**

The first known examples of a team game involving a ball, which was made out of a rock, occurred in old Mesoamerican cultures for over 3,000 years ago. It was by the Aztecs called Tchatali, although various versions of the game were spread over large regions. In some ritual occasions, the ball would symbolize the sun and the captain of the losing team would be sacrificed to the gods. A unique feature of the Mesoamerican ball game versions was a bouncing ball made of rubber – no other early culture had access to rubber.

The first known ball game which also involved kicking took place In China in the 3rd and 2nd century BC under the name cuju. Cuju was played with a round ball (stitched leather with fur or feathers inside) on an area of a square. A modified form of this game later spread to Japan and was by the name of kemari practiced under ceremonial forms.

Perhaps even older cuju was Marn Gook, played by Aboriginal Australians and according to white emigrants in the 1800s a ball game primarily involving kicking. The ball was made by encased leaves or roots. The rules are mostly unknown, but as with many other early versions of the game keeping the ball in the air was probably a chief feature.

Other variety of ball games had been known from Ancient Greece. The ball was made by shreds of leather filled with hair (the first documents of balls filled with air are from the 7th century). Ball games had, however, a low status and was not included at the Panhellenic Games. In the Ancient Rome, games with balls were not included in the entertainment on the big arenas (amphitheaters), but occurred in exercises in the military by the name of Harpastum. It was the Roman culture that would bring football to the British island (Britannica). It is, however, uncertain in which degree the British people were influenced by this variety and in which degree they had developed their own variants.

- **The game of football takes its form**

The most admitted story tells that the game was developed in England in the 12th century. In this century, games that resembled football were played on meadows and roads in England. Besides from kicks, the game involved also punches of the ball with the fist. This early form of football was also much more rough and violent than the modern way of playing.

An important feature of the forerunners to football was that the games involved plenty of people and took place over large areas in towns (an equivalent was played in Florence from the 16th century where it was called Calcio). The rampage of these games would cause damage on the town and sometimes death to the participants. These would be among the reasons for the proclamations against the game that finally was forbidden for several centuries. But the football-like games would return to the streets of London in the 17th century. It would be forbidden again in 1835, but at this stage the game had been established in the public schools.

It took, however, long time until the features of today's football had been taken into practice. For a long time there was no clear distinction between football and rugby. There were also many variations concerning the size of the ball, the number of players and the length of a match.

The game was often played in schools and two of the predominant schools were Rugby and Eton. At Rugby the rules included the possibility to take up the ball with the hands and the game we today know as rugby has its origin from here. At Eton on the other hand the ball was played exclusively with the feet and this game can be seen as a close predecessor to the modern football. The game in Rugby was called "the running game" while the game in Eton was called "the dribbling game".

An attempt to create proper rules for the game was done at a meeting in Cambridge in 1848, but a final solution to all questions of rules was not achieved. Another important event in the history of football came about in 1863 in London when the first Football association was formed in England. It was decided that carrying the ball with the hands wasn't allowed. The meeting also resulted in a standardization of the size and weight of the ball. A consequence of the London meeting was that the game was divided into two codes: association football and rugby.

The game would, however, continue to develop for a long time and there was still much flexibility concerning the rules. For one thing, the number of players on the pitch could vary. Neither were uniforms used to distinguish the appearance of the teams. It was also common with players wearing caps – the header was yet to be a part of the game yet. Further reading: The development of football rules.

Another important difference at this stage could be noticed between English and Scottish teams. Whereas the English teams preferred to run forward with the ball in a more rugby fashion, the Scottish chose to pass the ball between their players. It would be the Scottish approach that soon became predominant.
The sport was at first an entertainment for the British working class. Unprecedented amounts of spectators, up to 30,000, would see the big matches in the late 19th century. The game would soon expand by British peoples who traveled to other parts of the world. Especially in South America and India would the interest in football become big.

- **The first football clubs**

Football clubs have existed since the 15th century, but unorganized and without official status. It is therefore hard to decide which the first football club was. Some historians suggest that it was the Foot-Ball Club formed 1824 in Edinburgh. Early clubs were often formed by former school students and the first of this kind was formed in Sheffield in 1855. The oldest among professional football clubs is the English club Notts County that was formed in 1862 and still exists today.

An important step for the emergence of teams was the industrialization that led to larger groups of people meeting at places such as factories, pubs and churches. Football teams were established in the larger cities and the new railroads could bring them to other cities.In the beginning, football was dominated by public school teams, but later, teams consisting by workers would make up the majority. Another change was successively taking place when some clubs became willing to pay the best players to join their team. This would be the start of a long period of transition, not without friction, in which the game would develop to a professional level.

The motivation behind paying players was not only to win more matches. In the 1880s the interest in the game has moved ahead to a level that tickets were sold to the matches. And finally, in 1885 professional football was legalized and three years later the Football League was established. During the first season, 12 clubs joined the league, but soon more clubs became interested and the competition would consequently expand into more divisions.For a long time, the British teams would be dominant. After some decades, clubs from Prague, Budapest and Sienna would be the primarily contenders to the British dominance.

As with many things in history, women were for a long time excluded from participating in games. It was not before the late 19th century that women started to play football. The first official women's game took place in Inverness in 1888.

- **The first competitions**

Other milestones were now to follow. Football Association Challenge Cup (FA Cup) became the first important competition when it was run in 1871. The following year a match between two national teams was played for the first time. The match that involved England and Scotland ended 0-0 and was followed by 4,000 people at Hamilton Crescent (the picture shows illustrations from this occasion).

Twelve years later, in 1883, the first international tournament took place and included four national teams: England, Ireland, Scotland and Wales.Football was for a long time a British phenomenon, but it gradually spread to other European countries. The first game that took place outside Europe occurred in Argentina in 1867, but it was foreign British workers who were involved and not Argentinean citizens.

The Fédération Internationale de Football Association (FIFA) was founded in 1904 and a foundation act was signed by representatives from France, Belgium, Denmark, the Netherlands, Spain, Sweden and Switzerland. England and the other British countries did not join FIFA from the start, they had invented the game and saw no reason to subordinate to an association. Still, they joined in the following year, but would not partake in the World Cup until 1950.

Domestic leagues occurred in many countries. The first was, as already mentioned, the English Football League which was established in 1888. The leagues would by time expand by more divisions, which were based on team performance.In 1908 would football for the first time be included as an official sport in the Olympic Games. Until the first FIFA World Cup was played in 1930, the Olympic Games football tournament would rank as the most prestigious on a national level. Women's football was not added until 1996.

- **Black players**

As in many other sports the white male was predominant for a long time. In football black players started being present relatively early and in comparison with, for example, tennis, football has traditionally been known as a sport with a mix of black and white players.In Britain, Andrew Watson is known to be the first black player, and he played in the Scottish club Queen's Park in the 1880s.

- **A game of passion**

Few other sports show examples of passion to that extent as football. The arenas are flocked by shearing people and in front of television even more are watching carefully and sometimes with great enthusiasm. Already in the late 19th century, Goodison Park was built in England in purpose of hosting football games. In 1894, the FA Cup final between Notts County and Bolton Wanderers was attended by 37,000 people. A milestone in the development of football stadiums is the construction of Maracanã Stadium. In the year of 1950 the imposing stadium in Rio de Janeiro was ready for almost 200,000 people. No other sport has seen stadiums of that capacity built to host its games.

There have been two different traditions of fan culture on the arenas: the British and the South American. The British fans adopted the tradition of singing, the repertoire was inspired from pub and working songs among other areas. The South Americans on the other hand would adopt the carnival style which included firecrackers and fireworks, and also the modern phenomena of Bengali fires. Fans in other countries have later adopted a mixture of these traditions.

- **The great modern competitions**

No other sport event besides the Summer Olympic Games can today measure itself with the FIFA World Cup. The first edition of the FIFA World Cup was played in 1930 in Uruguay and has since then returned every fourth year (with two exceptions due to the Second World War). In 1991 the first World Cup for women was held in China and has since then also returned every fourth year.Today the biggest global tournament for clubs is the Champions League (played since 1992), the former European Cup (1955–1991).

- **Globalization of the biggest sport in the world**

In the late 19th century, only a few national football teams existed; England and Scotland had the first active teams that played games against each other in the 1870s. Today there are 211 national associations included in the Fédération Internationale de Football Association (FIFA), the world governing body of the sport. Another proof of the globalization could be seen in the increase of nations participating in the World Cup qualifiers: from 32 in 1934 to over 200 in 2014.

The world regions have been divided into six confederations: Confédération Africaine de Football (CAF), Asian Football

Confederation (AFC), Union des Associations Européennes de Football (UEFA), The Confederation of North, Central America and Caribbean Association Football (CONCACAF), Oceania Football Confederation (OFC), and Confederación Sudamericana de Fútbol (CONMEBOL).

THREE

HISTORY OF FOOTBALL STADIUMS

- **History of football stadiums**

Sport activities elicit fervent responses from people and the passion of players matches the excitement of spectators and fans. The global sporting industry is worth over $600 billion and with the amount of money circulating, major sport arenas boast impressive structures. Speaking of architecture some are more remarkable than others. But, how did football stadiums look originally? How did they evolve? Who are the individuals who changed the pitches from the set aside grass areas to properly maintained stadiums?

- **The first stadiums**

When Association Football was in its starting phase, people played their matches on spare playing fields, mostly within the public parks. The biggest worry of players was whether passers would understand exactly what was happening and have the courage to walk around the pitch.
With growth of football popularity and professionalism, the need to develop better grounds where players would like to be arose.

Football clubs started doing more than just brushing some debris off the grass and sending boys out for short matches. Ground that could be used for football and other games, like rugby, had existed for a while. The very first ground, Sandygate Road, opened already in 1804. Almost 60 years later, the first football match between Hallam and Sheffield FC was played here.

Initially, the markings seen on the local pitches were non-existent. Football pitches featured bollard or fence along the field edges to help players know where they could not go beyond and to keep the spectators closer. In addition to that, the fields featured two sticks, fundamentally, at each pitch end to represent the goals.

It might seem strange to hear that football pitches were the suitable looking grassy areas. In most cases, it was the ideal section of the public park – the straightest part. As the popularity of this game increased, teams started using private land. For example, Preston North End moved in 1875 to Deepdale to play its matches on a ground that was formerly a farm, and considering the initial state of the field, they encountered numerous problems.

- **Dunstable Road, the home for Luton Town FC 1897-1905.**

The period 1889-1910 marked a start of an era of numerous stadium constructions in England; fifty league clubs moved to new stadiums during this period. The stadiums were commonly built in centrum city areas - a circumstance that have created difficulties when the need for an expansion has arose much later.
The stadiums were relatively alike from an architectural aspect. They featured one or two covered grandstand and open terraces was filling out the rest of the oval form around the field.

The overcrowded stands in the late 19th centuries were a proof of the increased interest for the sport in England. In the early 20th century, enormous crowds were gathered in special occasions as finals in competitions. One such occasion was the 1913 FA Cup final played at Crystal Palace with over 120,000 spectators. The overcrowded stands would lead to the first recorded stadium disaster, which happened in 1902 when parts of a stand at Ibrox Park in Glasgow collapsed. The outcome was 25 killed and more than 500 injured. Football historian David Goldblatt writes in The Ball is Round: "The Ibrox disaster was driven by combination of enormous crowds, and a commercialism that sanctioned under-investment in shoddy infrastructure."

- **Development of football stadiums**

Before 1960, football pitches featured regular grass. Later in the 1980s, developers installed drainage systems in them. Originally, pitches required substantial amount of maintenance to keep them in the right shape. They were reliant on regular lighting and watering.

In the year 1958, people witnessed undersoil heating put underneath the football-playing surface in Goodison Park. The twenty miles – roughly thirty kilometers – wire was laid under the surface, costing the football club over £16,000. The purpose of this heating system was to prevent freezing on the pitch and was more effective than the installers thought. And because the ancient drainage system could not cope with the new water floods, the pitch was taken up and relaid in 1960 and better drainage systems installed.

Still, in the year 1960, people witnessed the introduction of first-generation artificial turf. The first-generation artificial turf was very different from the pleasant lifelike artificial grass on soccer pitches today. It was low-piles, stiff nylon fibers attached to asphalt or concrete bases. It was first installed in Astrodome Texas. Professional footballers encountered artificial turf when Luton Town, Queens Park Rangers, Oldham Athletic and Preston North

End introduced the second-generation turf to their fields in the year 1980. The United Kingdom government illegalized artificial turf in the year 1995.

- **The modern football stadiums**

In the year 2001, UEFA and FIFA started quality assurance programs for artificial turf development. That helped them come up with industry standards for its use in the soccer world. And as a result, the International Football Association Board tackled the problem of turf in the 2004 Laws of The Game.

4G pitches, also known as fourth generation pitches, came into being in the year 2010 and their popularity has been growing. The pitches are a hybrid of natural grass and artificial turf and people can therefore use them for a very long time without any sign of wear and tear. The increased popularity of turf results from the improved image of The John Smith's Stadium in Huddersfield.

Deesso Grassmaster pitches are now common in our stadiums, but were laid for the first time in 1996 in the home of Huddersfield Giants Rugby League Club and Huddersfield Town Football Club. The benefits of artificial and real turf hybrid are clear. Maintenance problems that were common in earlier days are no longer a big problem. Football pitches are not lit or watered regularly and groundskeepers can easily monitor them.

Football arenas such as Camp Nou in Barcelona, gives the sport events another dimension by their grandiose and spectacular framing.The stadiums have grown bigger and bigger, but on the same time the maximum attendances have decreased. The shift from standing places to seats has increase the safety a lot, but it also means that some old records, such as the 173,850 (unofficially, the attendance has been estimated to be over 200,000), at the Maracanã stadium the 16 July when Brazil played against Uruguay in 1950 World Cup will probably never be broken.

The shift to all-seater stadiums was a result of the Hillsborough disaster in 1989. A regulation stipulated that standing places should be removed completely on all Premier League venues before the start of the 1994-95 season. The same rules have been introduced in several other countries. FIFA and UEFA command nowadays all-seater stadiums for all their competitions.

- **The economic impact of stadium capacity**

The size of a football club's stadiums also reflects the revenues. A team with 30,000 capacity has a major handicap against a team with 60,000 capacity. The latter team can afford bigger players transfers and player wages. In Premier League, Manchester United's Old Trafford was for a long time superior to Arsenal's Highbury in this aspect. Arsenal though the disadvantage was enough critical to invest almost €400 million in a new stadium, which was the Emirates stadium that was ready in 2006. The same route was chosen by Tottenham. White Heart Lane had been their home for over a century, but the revenues from its 36,284 capacity couldn't match that of the other English top clubs. The solution was a gigantic investment that resulted in a plus 60,000 capacity stadium with a removable turf field.

A third factor, besides the amounts of fans that can be capsuled and the revenue aspects, is the symbolic and commercial value. A stadium is an important symbol for the team and when a new stadium is built it should look impressive. In many ways ... as Joshua Robinson and Jonathan Clegg puts it in The Club: "Arsenal's new stadium wouldn't just be a venue for 60,000 fans attending in person, it would be a backdrop for the 60 million watching around the world".Tottenham Hotspur Stadium is hard to miss if you are in the neighborhood.

Football stadiums gets enormous media exposure, which has opened win-win situations for owners and other companies. Several clubs have profited by given naming rights to companies that is willing to pay for the branding opportunity. Some examples are Allianz Arena (Allianz is a financial services company), Bet365 Stadium (if someone has missed it, Bet365 is a betting company), King Power Stadium (King Power Stadium is a travel retail group) and Vodafone Arena (Vodafone is a telecom company).

FOUR

THE EVOLUTION OF FOOTBALL SHOES

- **The evolution of football shoes**

Football shoes, also called cleats or soccer boots, are special footwear that is worn while playing football (soccer). They are specifically designed for the pitch and the cleats on the sole of the shoe aid the grip during the game. Football boots are by no means a new concept, but they have evolved throughout time thanks to technology and better research.

- **The Early Days**

Before the year 1891, football boots weren't in use. Instead, the players wore work boots. These were obviously hard to maneuver in and quite heavy on the foot. They weren't designed for people to run in or to kick a ball with. Furthermore, they usually had a reinforced toe, sometimes made of steel; this led to injuries whenever one player accidentally kicked another. They also didn't have any kind of additional grip since there was a regulation that footballers couldn't wear any shoes with anything sticking out from them.

A revision around 1891 allowed football shoes to utilize small bars or studs on the shoes. Soon after that, work boots were replaced with actual football boots designed with leather in order to better perform in the sport. They were made of thick leather and were still quite heavy (about 0.5kg dry and heavier if wet). They also laced up the ankle for better protection. This was the beginning of the modern football boots we know of today.

- **The 1900s**

The early decades of the 1900s saw little change for football shoes. The World Wars and their aftermaths left little materials for new creations and, frankly, with so many men involved in the war efforts, the demand for updated boots wasn't there. During this time, however, Valsport and Gola were the popular brands marketed to footballers.

After World War II developers and players took an interest in the sport and the footwear again. At this time, football boots began to change noticeably. New technology and research allowed developers to create flexible boots that were much lighter on the foot. The idea of protecting the players' feet took a backseat to the primary concern of better agility and performance. Besides being lighter, the new football boots also came up a little lower on the leg to improve flexibility. These lower boots were especially popular in places like Southern Europe and South America where conditions were less muddy than England.

In the 1950s, Adidas introduced their own football boot that came with screw-in studs that were interchangeable. The studs were either rubber or plastic and were specifically made to be used in different weather or field conditions. This meant that football players no longer had to have two different pairs of shoes, they could use one boot with interchangeable studs instead.

Over time, football boots became even lighter, but the real change came in their designs. Throughout the early years and into the mid-1900s the boots only came in black, but around the 1970s designers began to experiment with different colors. The material was going through a time of experiments and improvements as well. During this footwear revolution, the most popular and famous football boot was created. It was known as the Predator by Adidas. With rubber strips of the same material used a tennis bat in the top of the shoes the power and the amount of spin on the ball was increased. It was a worldwide sensation.It was also during this time that professional players were receiving endorsements to wear specific brands of football boots.

In the final years of the 1900s and into the new millennium football shoes evolved further in terms of the soles of the boots. The change came about as developers saw a need for more flexibility. Since there are cleats on the underside of football boots, they were a little stiff to best support the studs. The new developments during this time allowed for the soles to best support the cleats while providing better flexibility and a better range of motion. This evolution was done by most brands but Adidas's Predator still help the top position in terms of use and sales.

- **Present Day Trends**

Thanks to laser technology, football shoes are now able to be customized to best fit an individual's foot. This is a popular trend with professional footballers. Personalization is also a popular option nowadays. For example, professionals now choose to have their name and sometimes their jersey number on their customized boots. The studs were also updated to more of a blade for better grip on the pitch. Rubber and plastic studs are, however, still available. Further technological developments that are believed to continue as the sport grows in popularity are the use of microchips and tracking tools. These are small computerized devices that will be placed in the shoe and allow a player to track their movements and their performance either on a computer or on their smartphone.

- **Different Types of Shoes**

Up until now, all of the football boots that have been discussed have been for outdoor use. In addition, there are indoor football boots that are slightly different than the outdoor variety. The indoor football shoes are built to be used on flat, hard surfaces instead of a grass pitch. These boots have rubber soles with no studding so they have a better grip on hard floors.

It should also be noted that screw-in studs have fallen out of favor due to the frequency of stud-related injuries caused by the metal cleats. Football clubs, like Manchester United, have also issued bans on bladed boots after players were injured.

- **Shoes Brands**

Adidas was the most popular brand for a while, but nowadays there are a number of popular brands. Companies like Nike and Umbro compete right alongside Adidas with big name players endorsing the different brands. Thanks to these endorsements, Nike and Adidas seem to be the most popular brands of football boots with big stars like Cristiano Ronaldo promoting them on and off the pitch. Over the years, football shoes have taken on different sizes, shapes, and colors, but the main goal of developers have always been providing players with the best possible performance. As technology advances, you can be sure that football boots will continue to evolve, too.

Thank You

Thank You For Reading This Book. Shared This Book In Friends Birthday.

Printed by Libri Plureos GmbH in Hamburg,
Germany